THE RETIREMENT TRAP

Books by Leland Frederick Cooley and Lee Morrison Cooley

THE SIMPLE TRUTH ABOUT WESTERN LAND INVESTMENT
THE RETIREMENT TRAP

Novels by Leland Frederick Cooley
Member, Authors League of America

THE RUN FOR HOME
GOD'S HIGH TABLE
THE RICHEST POOR FOLKS

THE
RETIREMENT
TRAP

179

(by) Leland Frederick Cooley
and
Lee Morrison Cooley

DOUBLEDAY & COMPANY, INC.   GARDEN CITY, NEW YORK

1965

CONTENTS

citizens and what those needs will cost them in the immediate future.

For

HARRY MORRISON

who knew this
book was to be
for him.

And for

Rose Morrison

who shared so many
years with him.

1

TWO TRUE STORIES

Nothing can explain this book's purpose or its title more effectively than these two stories. Both are true.

Two families are involved. A.L. and his family live in Monterey, California. Z.K. and his family live in Miami, Florida. They have a great deal in common.

Both men are retired. Both men worked for themselves as retail merchants. Both made approximately the same annual income. Both bought average life, health, and accident insurance to protect their families. Both men planned for retirement and sold their businesses for a profit at age sixty-five. Both men have wives about five years younger than they, women in good health, who actively helped them plan for their leisure years. Both couples have two grown, married children and both couples have small grandchildren.

As this is written, A.L. is nearing his seventieth birthday. He is in robust good health and his last annual checkup would portend another decade of active life. That would seem to be the heritage left him by his own parents, both of whom lived well into their eighties.

A.L.'s gross estate is approximately $150,000. This includes $32,000 realized from the sale of an old family home. The money is invested in tax-free municipal bonds and in two savings and loan accounts that currently pay 4.85 per cent interest. There is $10,000 of paid-up life insurance. And there is a completely free and clear four-plex apartment house in the town of Monterey that produces an annual net income of just under $4000. Total spendable income is over $5000 a year.

A.L.'s estate is further protected by a health insurance plan purchased through his fraternal organization. It guarantees 80 per cent of the cost of most of the in and out of hospital treatment and services that a man and wife will encounter in their later years. A.L. said the premiums through the group plan are just about $200 a year. And there is a modest savings account.

All known factors considered it seems reasonable to suppose that A.L. and his wife will live out their "golden years" or their "sunset years" or their "leisure years" without too much tribulation and A.L.'s carefully planned estate will be distributed according to his wishes. But there is always that big IF—as we shall see in the story of Z.K.

His gross estate was $168,000. The cash value of his home, also without encumbrances at time of retirement, was $22,-500. The net proceeds after capital gains taxes on the sale of his business amounted to $103,000, which included a valuable piece of business property plus the installations and good will.

In addition there were two second mortgages worth $20,-000, each drawing 6 per cent annually and a savings account of $6200. The balance of the estate represented the cash value of two insurance policies, some jewelry, and a new car. Z.K.'s annual income was around $6000.

Then, two years ago, during a routine medical examination, it was found that Z.K. had a suspicious-looking growth beside his left kidney. The doctors did not feel that an operation was necessary at the time. They advised frequent examinations. Most of that cost was not defrayed by Z.K.'s health insurance policy since it was diagnostic investigation and not treatment for a specific disease. Those bills were paid out of savings. So were the doctor's fees.

After frequent examinations there seemed to be a significant change in the growth shown on the X-ray films. An operation was indicated.

So Z.K., apparently a well and active man, at sixty-eight, submitted to surgery. The pathological report verified an active cancer.

This time the policy helped. After the first $50 had been paid by Z.K.'s wife, the insurance paid a sizable percentage of the in-hospital expenses plus a surgical allowance. However, the payments covered only thirty-one days of care and Z.K. was in the hospital for over two months. Suddenly the bills were terrifying. A depression settled upon the patient and his family.

When Z.K. was finally allowed to go home his mental attitude improved somewhat. His wife took care of him during the day and a special nurse was engaged for night duty.

Several months passed, all filled with unusual expenses for nursing, medicine, and treatment. Although the surgeon felt reasonably certain that he had removed the entire growth, subsequent X-rays showed an adjacent area had become involved. A second operation was decided upon. Because a year had not elapsed, the insurance did not apply.

Within the year and a half since the examination first detected the cancer in the left kidney, all of the savings had been exhausted as well as the benefits under Z.K.'s health insurance.

When interviewed again several months later Mrs. Z.K. said that the two second mortgages had been discounted to a firm that purchases such paper at 15 per cent below its current face value. That cash was earmarked to pay for full-time care in a professional nursing home. There seems no reasonable possibility that Z.K. will improve and be able to return to his own home.

Also there seems no real possibility that the chain of events that are draining off capital at an alarming rate can be stopped.

With savings gone, hospital benefits exhausted under the insurance plan, and mortgages discounted to produce more cash, only time will tell whether or not enough will be salvaged to take care of Mrs. Z.K.

Every time it is necessary to spend capital the income from the remainder is reduced. The oftener the process is repeated the smaller the income that is left.

Such prospects are dreadful and most mortals are uncomfortable when confronted by them. They either refuse to admit the possibility or denounce as havoc-criers those who warn them.

As life lingers hopelessly and money dwindles ceaselessly both the victim and the family are caught in a tragic dilemma. Those who love the victim want, with all of their hearts, to keep him among the living. But in their minds they struggle against guilt-ridden hopes that death will come before impoverishment.

And the victim too, if he or she is aware of the true circumstances, is torn with emotion for so long as reason remains.

"If I could pray for others in my circumstances," said the seventy-eight-year-old widow of a retired man who had just died after a devastating lingering illness, "I would pray that all of the hopelessly ill die fast."

During conversations shortly after the doctors had spoken candidly of her husband's chances, Z.K.'s bewildered wife did some thinking aloud. She wondered why God had seen fit to visit such punishment on a man as good as her husband. And she wondered many other things. Understandably there was a touch of self-pity.

"I just don't know what we've done to deserve this. My son tells me now that we may have to borrow on the house. If my husband goes on living—and I pray to God he does if he's not suffering—then we may have to sell it, too."

The tears that had been just below the surface for months

came near brimming again as she added, "Believe me, I'm telling you the truth—this family is caught in a terrible trap!"

Despite all of the precautions we can take, all the sacrifices we can make to ensure our security, it is a matter of fact that today, in the most humane and abundant economy the world has ever known, *for most of us there is no absolutely certain way to achieve real security for ourselves and our loved ones from the cradle to the grave.*

Through one misfortune or another most of the 18.7 million over retirement age in 1965—will be caught in The Retirement Trap.

2

ERARE HUMANUM EST

We make mistakes in planning for retirement because we are human. And human beings are naturally and profoundly optimistic. If this were not so, mankind could never have survived its follies. Few of us ever consider that truly bad things will happen to us personally or to our loved ones. "Those grave misfortunes always happen to others," we say. And so we go along day by day occasionally feeling a tinge of worry or fear that the odds may catch up with us when some of the more vivid insurance advertisements cause us to stop a moment and take stock. But mostly we remain profit-motivated, freely enterprising bundles of confidence in "The American Dream" out to get our share from the golden grab bag of our seemingly inexhaustible economy.

Include in this company that small but increasing cadre of bona fide developers, energetic promoters, and outright con men who have appeared on the retirement scene with their blandishments, brochures, and bulldozers offering to erase most of the worry wrinkles from our "golden years" by building villages, towns, and skyscrapers in which all of the physical and spiritual needs of the senior citizens among us may allegedly be met for a modest fee each month—after the normal down payment.

There is nothing very wrong with the best of them—as far as they go. And there are serious things wrong with the worst of them. The largest of them are profit-motivated. The most numerous of them are, or claim to be, nonprofit organizations, many of which claim direct relationship to one religious sect or another. A pitiful few of them—far too few—are federal, city, and state joint ventures in low-cost, subsidized housing for the very poor. The best of this latter group point the way to at least a partial chance of escape for some of the trapped elders. New York City's low-cost housing is an outstanding example. The city of Cleveland has written a bright and hopeful new page in low-cost housing. So has Denver, and Reno, Nevada's Tom Sawyer Village is one of the most promising projects in the country—an admirable starting point for smaller cities.

There is no accurate census of the number of low-income elders being sheltered comfortably in city housing authority projects throughout the nation, but it seems unlikely that more than a half million persons will have found such facilities available by the end of 1965.

This means the majority of senior citizens will still be forced to make out as they always have, as unwilling dependents of children or as lonely outcasts in substandard housing.

In government there has been an acute awareness of the seriousness and magnitude of the problem of adequate care for the older people in this country who have been forced into retirement by industries with no further need for them or by illnesses that render them unfit to compete in the labor market. It was this awareness that inspired the creation of the President's Council on Aging on May 14, 1963. In his special message to Congress in which he explained the need for retirement housing and health care, President Kennedy said, *"A proud and resourceful nation can no longer ask its older people to live in constant fear of a serious illness for which adequate funds are not available. . . . We owe them the right of dignity in sickness as well as in health. We can achieve this by adding health insurance—primarily hospitalization insurance—to our successful social security system."*

The statement was no sooner made than a storm of protest rose from private enterprise. "Socialized medicine" was the dreaded label affixed to the young president's proposal and the reaction from the American Medical Association and private insurance interests was instantaneous and vocal.

In insurance circles there was an accelerated move to revise health policies. Within a very short time new hospitalization and surgical plans were being advertised in full-page spreads across the nation aimed at the senior citizen retirement market, a market whose total income is $40 billion—a huge market that hitherto had remained almost overlooked.

Private building industry also began to sit up and take notice. Long preoccupied with the herculean task of providing conventional housing for our exploding population, it had paid little if any attention to this special senior segment of the housing market until President Kennedy spotlighted it and its pressing needs. This sort of housing usually has been left to the various government agencies and to the metropolitan housing authorities of the big cities. But even to an industry long accustomed to astronomical market figures, a $40 billion market was a pluck-worthy plum.

Suddenly there was a general awakening to a number of special sections set up under the Federal Housing Authority to evaluate and insure huge private loans made for the purpose of supplying housing for senior citizens. The building industry had been aware for some time that church-sponsored or -initiated groups had been securing multimillion-dollar private loans insured by the Federal Housing Authority for the purpose of erecting so-called nonprofit housing developments for older people. When developers, builders, and promoters dug into the figures and verified the sound economics of the market they found insurance companies, savings and loan institutions, and some banks waiting at the curb to lend billions that could be safely insured by Uncle Sam up to 90 per cent and even 100 per cent of the cost of the project.

Almost overnight surveyors and earth movers appeared in

remote mountain valleys, in cotton fields, alfalfa fields, bean fields, and cow pastures from ten to a hundred miles from the downtown areas of a dozen principal cities in the four corners of the country.

Subsequently eager land · buyers with generous option money rushed up to the owners of every likely piece of property from eight to 80,000 acres in size and attempted, often successfully, to secure sites for still more.

But like all of these gold-rush operations, the first prospectors have been so eager to get rich quick that they have concentrated their efforts on staking claims in the obvious locations. There is some evidence now that the richest exposed portions of the mother lode of retirement building have been taken up and the second wave of prospectors eagerly pressing in may have to search farther and mine deeper for their share of the $40 billion bonanza.

This book will look at the *human side* of this great new retirement problem. As a market it has been analyzed in terms of dollars and cents by a thousand experts and we will leave the endless columns of figures to them. Purchasing power comes from people. Our interest is in the problems of people.

Even for those few favored souls who will have total security in their retired years, retirement itself poses some very vexing problems. For the well-to-do the problems are almost entirely emotional. For the great majority of the potential victims of the retirement trap, however, there is not just one problem or even two or three. There are a score of problems, emotional, financial, and physical.

Again, no one was more cognizant of the complicated nature of these problems than President John Kennedy. This was revealed in another passage of his special message to Congress when he said, *"The heart of our program for the elderly must be opportunity for and actual service to our older citizens in their home communities. The loneliness or apathy which exists among many of our aged is heightened by the wall of inertia which often exists between them and their community."*

The President was too considerate to call that inertia by its right name—indifference—the indifference that too often exists in the hearts of the preoccupied younger ones toward their own elderly.

In hundreds of interviews with retired persons in their old family homes, in the new retirement villages and towns and in institutions, we found that *the great need—indeed the transcendent need of the older person—is the need to be needed.*

So, these pages will examine this leisure that comes with retirement. They will look at its blessings and its problems. They will look at it in many places in the nation. The reader will see that too often leisure's companions are loneliness and fear. The reader will hear what retired persons in every walk of life think about enforced leisure, about fixed incomes, and about the new retirement communities with all of their opportunities for group activities and recreation. And the reader will discover whether or not such activities really do the job of warding off loneliness and providing companionship and love—and whether or not our whole new concept of retirement living is meeting or failing to meet the true, deep-seated need for security and a useful place in a society that soon will consist of 30 per cent young and 30 per cent old people. As often as possible the nature of The Retirement Trap will be described in the actual words of those people who are now caught in it or who are desperately trying to avoid it.

3

THE PROSE AND THE CON

"I may be sixty-five, son, but by gosh, I'm not ready to be tagged a 'senior citizen!'"

Thus spoke a nettled old duffer who was kind enough to interrupt his golf game on the third green of the course that meanders invitingly through the new retirement community.

Though he did not intend to, our friend was speaking for the majority of older Americans who have reached senior status. Actually they do not mind acknowledging that some sort of practical designation should be adopted to identify their economic and age group. What they really resent is the use of a designation that sounds like a *destination*.

"When they call us 'senior citizens' they don't leave us any place to go. It may be that we've about reached the end of the line. But we don't want to be reminded of it. You younger people are gonna be downright surprised some day to find out just how precious a year can be when it might very well be your last one!"

It took a while for the developers of retirement communities to understand what was going on—or rather what was not going on—when the older people who should have been flocking to stake out claims in some of these interim paradises were actually staying away in force because they had been offended by the phony, unctuous, unrealistic approaches that patronizing copywriters thought were "sure fire."

It is not known just who caught the mistake first. Back files seem to indicate that it was the Del E. Webb group, creators of the justly celebrated but occasionally damned Sun Cities in Arizona, California, and Florida.

In any case it soon became evident that the words "senior citizen" were anathema, and in the twinkling of a computer the great drive was on to corner the market in synonyms and euphemisms.

There followed, in full-page ads across the nation, a veritable avalanche of adjectives all adhesively modifying a host of new nouns and the whole concoction conveniently sloganized for instant use.

Through the miracle of letterpress and linotype the damage was offset or repaired with such alluring labels affixed to retirement or the retired as the New Leisure Set, the Golden Years, the Keepers of the Golden Years, the Holiday Years, the Friendly Years, the Relaxed Years, the Rewarding Years, and so ad infinitum. In one public relations firm, retirement community advertisements have been given the generic label Ads Nauseam.

But, no matter how much these selling techniques may antagonize some of the younger sophisticates, they have apparently hypnotized a sizable segment of our affluent elderly into plunking down everything from a modest monthly rental plus recreation-club dues to their entire estates for the privilege of living out at least a part of their leisure years in a state that seems to lie somewhere between Utopia and euphoria.

However, a visit to most of the important and typical retirement facilities in the nation will convince one that the real sales appeal lies not in the labels and slogans and carefully coifed and girdled middle-aged models who pose for the four-color brochures, but rather in a cleverly devised subliminal appeal that generates its real power from those installations which we call the *money magnets*.

What are *money magnets*? Very simply they are the Olympic-sized swimming pools, the eighteen-hole championship golf courses, the riding stables, and the truly fabulous club-houses and activities buildings that are invariably erected either slightly before or simultaneously with the model homes from which the development will be sold.

Men such as Del E. Webb and Ross Cortese have spent millions on these installations alone. Their appeal is undeniable—even to those far too young to qualify as purchasers. A little later it will be explained why those millions spent on the *money magnets* may very well have served another, unexpected and very vital, function that the developers did not even dream of when they conceived their retirement communities.

From the beginning though, these really stunning installations have done more to break down sales resistance than all of the ads, broadsides, and blandishments put together. And the reason is simple: They have said—in more than words—that each one of the prospective customers can enjoy a sort of pseudo country-club life that heretofore was available only to the very wealthy. But more importantly, these pools and golf courses, and tennis courts and riding stables have reinforced in most of the past-middle-age prospects the hope and the subjective conviction that, while some of their contemporaries may no longer be equal to the challenge, they still are. And feeling equal to that challenge is a very acceptable substitute for feeling young.

Listen to them as they comment on their new diversions:

"Well, I don't think I'd care to use the high diving board. But I'll betcha I can still swim ten laps—soon as I get some of the knots shaken out." Or:

"I used to be quite a swimmer when I was a kid but I haven't had much chance to stay in practice until now."

The odds are, however, that these same Mitty-ish Sammy Lees and Weissmullers who look with disdain at the nearby Jacuzzi hydrotherapy pool will be only too happy to sit in it for a half hour each day after they've found out just how far it is from one end to the other of an Olympic-sized swimming pool. But the challenge is there and their acceptance of it is the next to the last step before signing on the dotted line.

Nor should one underestimate the importance of these things to the ladies. They look at the ceramic room and the art studio and the sewing room and the card rooms and they succumb to the same subliminal appeal and respond to the same subjective challenge.

If all of these eager ladies followed through on first resolves to make hand-painted china or run up a few little dresses, even the low-cost Japanese labor could not hold out against the flood of crockery and frocks that would inundate the world market. Fortunately for all concerned that time-honored repository of good intentions still has plenty of pavable space left in it and the delicate balance of world trade is in no immediate danger. But the initial force of their enthusiasm is formidable and it is by consciously harnessing and guiding this force that the new advertising campaigns have compiled a record for effective selling that had not been equaled in any other segment of the home-building industry until developers competing for the younger family market suddenly woke up and began stealing pages from the retirement community sales book.

So-called *active retirement* is effecting a revolution in living habits across the entire spectrum of American suburban life. Because of the successful start being made by such organizations as the General Development Corporation, the Mackle Brothers, Del E. Webb, Ross Cortese, the University of Arizona Foundation, Alcan-Pacific, Pacific Coast Properties, Syar Inc., Boswell-Alliance Corporation, and others, it is better than an even bet that some 70 million members of the upcoming young adult generation will live more graciously, more sensibly, more economically, and more happily than any previous generation in our country's history.

Builders were quick to see that the grown children of the seniors who came to look at the retirement towns were as taken with the *money magnets* as their parents. A quick look

at the real estate section of any large Sunday paper will convince anyone that the young adults also mean to have all, or
most all, of these accouterments of country-club living. And
with more and more leisure time available to them under contracts calling for shorter work weeks and higher income, there
is no question that their wishes will be served.

Hollywood celebrities who long ago had shown interest in
lending their names and their money to various developments
have already entered the retirement field in some force as will
be seen in future chapters. But among the stars it remained
for Tennessee Ernie Ford to pioneer in the same sort of comprehensive living community for the younger set.

· Ford, in collaboration with developer Frederick Von Musser, has opened The Tennessean in Santa Ana, California.
Predictably, he and Musser have included all of the standard
money magnets. There seems little question that he is going to
find an enthusiastic reception by those too young to qualify
for the senior communities but who insist upon having comprehensive recreational facilities at a modest price.

4

THE FRIGHTENING FACTS

It is almost impossible to reduce human needs to statistics. Actually the needs of the retirees increase as their years increase and their incomes decrease. There are no dependable figures available that either enumerate or evaluate those increasing needs except in the most general terms. These needs vary with the individual retiree as indeed do all of the problems of all retirees with the exception of the two constants, the need to be needed, and the ever-present fear of lingering illness, total dependency, and death.

The older people among us are never very far from the brink of the Valley of the Shadow. As they pass sixty-five and move into their seventies the spectre of death is inescapable as friend after friend departs the scene.

The retirement communities offer little to allay such fears. Nor can they. The very concentration of the aging and aged sharpens the awareness and heightens the fear.

The many recreational and avocational diversions that are offered do a fair job of turning thought away from these fears for a time. But after the fun is over each evening, the fearsome spectres are back at their old haunts again.

How difficult it is for those who are still well and active and in the prime productive years to really understand or even believe that, for most active men, retirement is a traumatic experience. And how difficult it is for a younger woman who still has a vital husband to understand the unvoiced terror in the heart of the older wife who knows that the law of probabilities will almost certainly leave her a widow, more often than not dependent or partially dependent upon family, friends, or perhaps even on strangers.

These are not pleasant prospects. Most of the senior citizens interviewed admitted that, until it was no longer possible to avoid facing the facts of later life, they had gone on living day-to-day with their heads buried in the sand.

"But as the sands ran out there was no longer any time to hide," said Mrs. Grace Givens in the restaurant at Del Webb's Sun City near Riverside, California. "This is the place I'd like to live in. But after looking I'm not sure I can afford it without some help from my daughter—which is the one thing I'm hoping to avoid."

It was not that Sun City was expensive. On the contrary. It was that Mrs. Givens's fixed income suddenly looked minuscule compared to the income she had learned to live on during her late husband's top earning years.

At age sixty-six, Mrs. Givens can look forward to a fixed income of $240 a month. During the last twenty years of her husband's life she could depend upon at least $1000 a month with windfall bonuses each Christmas. But even at an average of $14,000 a year, the Givens family was unable to accumulate more than life insurance, the money to purchase a comfortable home outside of Elm Grove, Wisconsin, and two residential lots in a suburb of Milwaukee which had been sold under the terms of Mr. Givens's will so that the money could be reinvested to return a trickle of cash income.

In hundreds of interviews the story was always the same—insurance benefits meeting immediate emergencies—real estate forming the basis of a capital reinvestment plan—often in insurance—occasionally in the stock market. But invariably the result was a severely curtailed income, a frightening period of readjustment at a time of life when readjustments are most difficult.

Most of us are inclined to minimize the magnitude of this problem both in terms of the numbers who must face it and the degrees of difficulty in the solution. In the case of the latter, no figures exist that can measure the full scope of fear or plumb the depths of loneliness and despair. However, there are a great many dependable but rapidly changing figures extant that can give us a relatively accurate picture of the numbers of persons who are now, or who will soon be, facing the many problems of retirement.

For instance:

- There are *two* distinct generations of senior citizens.

  One out of three persons aged sixty has a living parent or relative over eighty.

- The 18.7 million senior citizens today are those who are sixty-five and over. They are nearly 10 per cent of our total population.

  We are adding to their numbers at the rate of 400,-000 annually.

- In 1900 there were three million over sixty-five years of age.

  In 1964 there were 18 million, an increase of 600 per cent.

- In 1964 there were 25 million persons over fifty-nine years of age and 21 million persons over sixty-two.

  By 1980 those over sixty-two years of age will number 30 million.

- At present, nearly half of the 18.7 million senior citizens over sixty-five are single.

  Of these, over 70 per cent are single women, widows, or maiden ladies.

· The average senior couple sixty-five years and older has an income of $2530 a year. Because it is an *average* figure the federal government assumes that half of the elderly couples have less than that figure and half of them have more.

· The average older citizen living alone is assumed to have an annual income of only $1055.

· Because these figures are averages one is tempted to accept the fact that of the persons sixty-five and over, 9.35 million of them are in dire straits and the other 9.35 million have it relatively easy. Nothing could be farther from the truth! Only one out of eighty-five had an income of $20,000 or more. Fewer than 50,000 had an income of $50,000 or more. Averages notwithstanding, the great majority of seniors exist on incomes well below these misleading *averages*.

While it is a fact that personal income from all sources, private and government, has increased substantially in the past decade, it is equally true that inflation and the high concentration of seniors in urban communities where living costs are higher have conspired to reduce the effectiveness of the increase. In short, the older people with fixed incomes have felt the inflation squeeze even more acutely than the others since they have less income and because they have greater needs for medicine and medical care, an area in which increases have been one of the greatest in the economy.

The figures go on and on. They measure, however inexactly, the growing urgency of a problem that is now upon this country. It is an economic problem and, as President Kennedy said, a moral problem too.

It is also an opportunity. But it is a double-edged one. For private enterprise it is an opportunity to demonstrate dramatically our economy's great vitality and flexibility and its ability to meet challenges with responsible action. For the advocates of more and more socialism it is a golden opportunity to put into action, with public money, many of their untried theories.

With populations exploding all over the world, other countries are watching the effectiveness with which our free enterprise society meets the challenge of responsible planning for the rapidly growing segment of our population that can no longer find a place in industry and business.

Those who say that federally conceived, financed, and administered retirement cities and a medical plan tied to our Social Security mechanism are the only practical answer have hurled a direct challenge to those who say that there is already too much government supervision of the individual's life . . . that big government begets bigger government with ever larger bureaucracies blossoming everywhere.

There is some truth in the argument. But there are inconsistencies in it too. For instance, much of the criticism leveled against expanding government emanates from the very men who appear before their stockholders to justify increasing capital expenditures or moratoriums on dividends on the plea that such measures are necessary to meet the challenge of our expanding population and the resultant expanding markets.

Markets are expanding in two ways: by using a superior product and competitive price to attract a larger segment of an existing market, and by the normal process of accrual through a population increase which expands the total market.

As may be seen from the over-all figures, few markets in the country are expanding as rapidly as the senior citizen market. And few markets have more numerous and more complicated needs, or more limited resources with which to meet those needs.

This is both the opportunity and the challenge—for government—and for private industry. The manner in which the opportunity is exploited will, in the next decade, profoundly affect the entire pattern of American social and economic life.

5

GOLD AMONG THE
SILVER THREADS

Total income figures for Americans sixty-five years of age and over vary greatly depending upon the government source. The report of the President's Council on Aging dated May 14, 1963, states that in 1950 there were 12.3 million Americans sixty-five and over with a total income of about $15 billion, while the 17 million citizens sixty-five and over in 1961 had a total income of $35 billion. The best projection on those figures showed a senior population of 18.7 million persons in 1965 with a total income from all sources of about $40 billion.

And still if one uses other income figures from that same report, and from the Bureau of Census, based on the income figures given in the previous chapter, it is difficult to arrive at a total income for our citizens sixty-five years of age and older of more than $30 billion. Whatever the actual figure may be— and nobody in Washington would pin one down—the senior American controls a lot of purchasing power and that power is growing.

While few of these dollars will go for luxuries, even in a luxury-minded economy, more of them will reach the market place than the dollars earned by the younger people in our economy who have swelled personal savings of all sorts to record highs.

The senior citizen's dollar must be spent. It will go for food,

clothing, lodging, medicine, and medical care. Precious little
of it will escape into other less necessary channels.

But there are markets within markets. The 200,000 elders
with incomes in excess of $20,000 annually have increased to
well over a quarter of a million. The 50,000 elders with incomes in excess of $50,000 annually have increased too,
though not proportionately because of taxes. But recent tax
reforms will tend to swell the spendable income of seniors in
the well-fixed brackets and increase the size of the market
accordingly. Depending upon the sources, figures may be had
to show a highly profitable retiree market of from five to eight
million persons with annual incomes in excess of $5000.

In a booklet edited by Beverly Diamond of the National
Council on the Aging, Martin E. Segal, President of Martin E.
Segal & Company, New York City, estimates that by 1975 this
new senior citizen market could show a gross annual income
of $55 billion. One official of the Census Bureau, using an
"educated guess based on still later projections," raised that
figure to $60 billion! No small part of this huge projected
increase is attributed to rapidly increasing Social Security
payments and to private pension fund reserves expected to
reach $100 billion or better by 1975.

It does not take much imagination to envision the power of
a senior citizen market in America with the benefits from these
huge funds at its disposal. Most economists agree that while
elderly people tend to cling to their savings and other investments because of a well-founded fear of catastrophic illness
generally not covered in insurance policies, nonetheless they
spend nearly all of their regular benefit checks without timidity
because they know they'll be receiving them for life.

During 1962, before the building industry really had a fair
chance at it, only seven promoters of retirement communities
in the East, South, and West had tapped the market for a gross
revenue of some $300 million. Their average net profit was
said to be close to 5 per cent.

Figures released by the Federal Housing Administration,

Division of Research and Statistics, for March 17, 1964, showed a total of 244 active projects insured under its Section 231. These projects encompassed 41,714 residential units for senior citizens with gross insurable mortgages totaling well over a half billion dollars.

These FHA figures *do not* take into account six huge retirement developments being undertaken in four states by Ross Cortese's Rossmoor Corporation, insured under Section 213 of the FHA. Nor do they include the activities of the Del E. Webb Corporation with its highly successful Sun Cities, all privately financed without insurance assistance from the FHA.

This then is a revealing glimpse at the size of the prime market at which the builders of retirement communities are aiming. It is estimated to have a potential of $25 billion!

Within the past three years, catering to the needs of our affluent elderly has made several new American millionaires from among the ranks of the giant building and land-development firms now engaged in an all-out struggle for what they feel is their fair share of those billions.

The paens of praise their advertising people have written may be heard on radio and may be seen on television and in the real estate sections of the nation's metropolitan press and in the extravagant brochures which seek to elevate the average retired person to a luxury status comparable to that of the old Palm Beach millionaires. Indeed, the best of the retirement communities furnish the senior citizen better and more varied recreation facilities than those old millionaires ever had.

As of the beginning of 1965, projects devoted in whole or in part to housing the senior citizen were under way in all but five of the fifty states with several important ones under construction in Washington, D.C., and in Puerto Rico.

All of the riches mined in California during the Gold Rush amounted to $2.75 billion. Remember then that the value of the retirement housing market is more than ten times that amount—a far from varicose vein and one well worth mining!

The old axiom "You get what you pay for" still holds. In

the retirement market it is especially true. But only the affluent elderly have a tremendous choice, ranging from small CBS (cement block-stucco) houses in Florida costing $6990 to swank, luxury rental units in Santa Monica, California's high-rise Ocean House with a monthly fee of $1100.

One of the principal reasons the retirement market has increased so spectacularly lies in the fact that a great number of developers are now turning their attention to a lower-age-higher-income bracket. Roughly, this expands the market to include everyone from forty-five on up. It is a richer market, one to whom the country-club aspect of retirement living has a greater appeal. A large percentage of the buyers still work. In effect this will increase the adult community market to approximately 20 per cent of the total population by 1970.

"Adult community" is a label to watch. The frantic search for acceptable synonyms and euphemisms that began when builders discovered that the nation's senior citizens do not like to be labeled as such has already been noted. After nearly two years of testing, most of the advertising men are agreed that "adult community" is the most effective label for these new developments.

The developers had another reason to think twice about the senior citizen and retirement village concept, but most of them deny it; the church-initiated or church-inspired, nonprofit, tax-exempt developers have been far and away the largest exploiters of the true senior-retirement market. They have been at it longer and despite the naïve claims and handy rationalizations that they often *spend more* and therefore must *charge more* because they are really only amateurs trying to fill a need, they have generally done a hardheaded business job. (In a subsequent chapter the activities of these so-called nonprofit, religiously inspired retirement communities will be examined both from a moral and material standpoint.)

Several big builders in Florida and in California have passed by the pure retirement market that is insurable under the FHA because they feel that federal supervision is too stringent and the market in those two leading retirement states is close to being saturated. Boyd Prior, Vice-president of marketing and sales for the General Development Corporation, Miami, Florida, said, "We feel there is a greater need for a broader community in which there are special facilities for the older residents but a community which appeals to the preretirement group as well." General Development's Port Charlotte on the Gulf coast has attracted a somewhat older group of buyers. Although it is not strictly a retirement city it probably contains the largest per capita concentration of retirees of any residential-recreational community in the country. On the other hand, Port St. Lucie on the Atlantic coast, just north of the Stuart-Jensen Beach-Rio area, seems to be attracting a somewhat younger, more affluent group of buyers. Both of these communities—only two of five major self-contained cities being built by General Development—seemed to be doing an admirable job of meeting the needs of a broad segment of the huge, new, adult housing market.

One of the most dramatic answers to the question "How big is big?" may be found in the completed plans for Del Webb's Sun City near Riverside, California. In a little over two years the retirement community has grown to approximately 4000 population. In the next two decades, the Del Webb management projects a Sun City population of 100,000. This means that in less than twenty-five years Sun City will have become as large as nearby Riverside, which will have taken over a century to accomplish the same growth![1]

For all those who must supply the thousands of services required by a full-blown city—retirement city though it may be —there is indeed a lot of gold among those silver threads!

[1] For the dramatic story of Riverside's founding and growth, read "The Simple Truth about Western Land Investment" by these same authors.

6

UTOPIA OR EUPHORIA?

With retirement, as in the parable of the blind men and the elephant, what one sees depends upon what one feels.

A thinking, feeling person cannot visit the scores of housing projects filled with older people patiently enduring what we call "the long wait," without being angered that so little is being done in areas where so much remains to be done.

For those persons whose incomes are at or just above the theoretical "modest but average" annual budget of $3010 established by the Bureau of Labor Statistics there is only moderate difficulty with adequate retirement housing in most areas.

For those seniors whose incomes exceed $20,000 a year, there is no problem at all—*IF they have made provision for the probability of a long terminal illness that can and usually does deplete an estate*. With reasonable planning most of them can avoid retirement's most vicious trap—total dependency.

Most of the others whose incomes are below the bare minimum established by the Bureau of Labor Statistics are, to one degree or another, already victims of The Retirement Trap.

Of course, there are always exceptions. The most favored to escape are those whose pensions and insurance are comprehensive enough to cover almost every exigency. GI insurance, fraternal organization insurance, union pensions and insurance, and certain types of annuity benefits are those most likely to furnish adequate protection. But here again, the coverage is small when compared to the needs of the total number of retired persons. Presently constituting 10 per cent of our population, our older Americans are projected to double in number the next two decades: 13.5 million of them are drawing Social Security benefits; 2.3 million of them have Veteran benefits. But in just five more years another 45 million Americans will be reaching retirement age. Figures are cold and impersonal. But the human problems concealed in them are staggering.

Except in the cases of those persons whose means were such that even a protracted illness would not seriously deplete their capital, every person interviewed confessed sooner or later that they simply did not dare allow themselves to think of the dire possibilities. A composite of their individual statements would read something like: "We can't do anything about it so there's no use worrying about it until it happens. Meanwhile we might as well eat, *not think,* and be merry!"

And so these retirement communities with their golden promises, their modestly priced down payments, their lavishly decorated model houses and apartments, their Olympic swimming pools and all of the other trappings of this new industry— the attractions we call *"money magnets"*—supply for the middle- and upper-middle-income groups of retirees a pleasant local anesthetic that deadens for a time at least the painful truth that inevitably will confront most of us.

Few enterprises in recent years have spent more money and energy to capture a new market than Del E. Webb with his Sun Cities, Ross Cortese with his Leisure Worlds, the Mackle Brothers with their new Deltona development in Florida, the General Development Corporation with its several "Port" cities, the vast Rancho Bernardo suburb of San Diego or the Tucson Green Valley "total community" initiated by a University of Arizona retirement foundation in collaboration with Maxon and Hunkin-Conkey construction companies of Cleveland.[1] In every sense of the word, these are new cities.

[1] $12,500,000 of the Tucson Green Valley, Arizona, financing is being provided by the New York State Teachers' Retirement System. This fact alone might lead to the logical assumption that before long The Westward Tilt, as author Neil Morgan puts it, will be inclined a few more degrees!

No developers have exceeded Ross Cortese and Del Webb
in the variety and lavishness of their *money magnets* which
are already so successful that in some instances lesser developers find they cannot compete without lowering the entrance
age still more to broaden the market of prospects. In doing
this they are forced to abandon their original concept of a retirement community for adults of fifty-two and over. A great
many now say, "No children under fifteen years of age," and
several, including actor Joe E. Brown's favorite development
at Port Hueneme, California, lowered this restriction to include children twelve years of age.

There is no question that in the most spectacular of the retirement cities the recreation and hobby facilities are a smash-
ing success in the sales office.

Older couples touring Sun City near Phoenix and at three
of the Leisure Worlds made no effort to conceal the wonderment on their faces. The same expressions are seen on the faces
of visitors touring the great sound stages in Hollywood's make-
believe world.

Once these curious seniors are in the *money magnet's* field
of attraction, very few of them escape! And this is one of the
reasons why the sales forces in most of these retirement communities are relatively small: a major portion of the softening-
up process has been accomplished by letting the prospects
wander at will through carefully defined areas and along carefully prescribed paths. Often they are speeded on their way
aboard private trams or buses that tend to camouflage the true
distances to the actual areas where their homes or apartments
will be built.

No prospect who enters the walled sales compounds may
leave without running the gauntlet of smiling, well-mannered,
and skillful sales psychologists lined up between him and the
door of the sales office. Even those who leave without buying
have not really escaped.

The rapturous looks one sees are not only on the faces of
the elders who are wondering at this new way of life. They

are also on the faces of the grown children of these elders who often accompany their parents on their shopping tour.

This may be called the *double-pull effect* of the *money magnets*. Not only do the younger couples see a relatively inexpensive and undeniably attractive place to pasture their aging parents, but they also see a chance to pay frequent visits, and for a nominal fee—often no fee at all—enjoy all of the recreation facilities, the least of which exceeds the average upper-crust country club.

"If these be pastures for the 'tended herds' [as Dr. Joseph H. Peck calls them] then let's start getting Ma and Pa tended right away!" you can almost hear them saying.

One salesman at Leisure World revealed that in a surprising number of cases the younger people do the "closing" for him. "All I have to do is present the contracts and take the down-payment check."

As we have seen, this eagerness of the younger members of the family to enjoy the first-rate country-club facilities their parents will have at hand has been seized upon by a number of builders who have all but abandoned the pure retirement concept in favor of the new, cluster-planned residential suburban communities with their variety of single dwellings, apartment and condominium town houses, all arranged in parklike surroundings and close to community centers offering everything from horseshoe courts to championship golf courses. In many of these, as in Rancho Bernardo and Lake San Marcos in Southern California, special areas have been set aside for seniors of fifty and over complete with their own recreation facilities and clubhouses.

Builders call these the new "age-integrated" cluster-planned suburbs and hail them as the fulfillment of the utopian concept of metropolitan living.

Certainly this tendency toward cluster planning can be a great blessing to metropolitan areas in the future. Not only is rapidly disappearing suburban land being made to accommodate more dwelling units, but this is being accomplished so

ingeniously that there is actually far more open park and recreation space preserved for the use of the residents.

Very soon now, as planning and building codes begin to
reflect an awareness of the benefits of this new land usage, we
can expect to see an end to the old grid-pattern developments
laid out in dull, unimaginative, and wasteful blocks of nearly
identical houses. Within another generation or two, real beauty
may return to the suburbs. *In no small degree will these residential development planners and builders owe this exciting
new concept to the pioneers in the retirement community field.*

It is difficult to say where the adult community concept
really began. Perhaps it was in Paradise, California, back in
the early 1930s. But most builders agree that the concept did
not really emerge clearly until Del E. Webb laid out his first
retirement community at Sun City near Phoenix, Arizona.

It would seem that most so-called revolutionary concepts
are really *evolutionary* concepts, with each developer taking
the best from some competitor, improving, embellishing, adding, until by now most of the practical improvisations on the
ancient village green plan have been extended to the limit of
economic practicability. Be that as it may, the process has resulted in an exciting variety of living and recreational choices
for the consumer with the cash or credit needed to pay his admission to Utopia. Small wonder then that some salesmen
in these new suburbs and retirement communities make as
much as $40,000 a year!

We know from personal experience the powerful pull of
those gleaming *money magnets*. We have felt it ourselves and
we have seen it at work on our neighbors. We live in Laguna
Beach, California, one of the most beautifully situated towns
along the entire Pacific shore. Set as they are on the steep
Riviera-like hillsides overlooking a necklace of cliff-set crescent
beaches, there is hardly a house that does not command a
spectacular view. And still, of the first six hundred applicants
to the Laguna Hills Leisure World—on the *inland* side of the
hills a good five miles from the ocean—*four hundred of them*

came from Laguna Beach! When the news got around, the town fathers were stunned. It seemed impossible to them that anyone in his right mind would desert a world-famous art colony with a world-famous climate and view for the hot, barren, inland side of the coastal hills, thousands of vacant acres that only two years ago were grazing land for herds of white-faced cattle.

Some of the town fathers discovered why when they saw what Ross Cortese's organization had provided—facilities that no town the size of Laguna Beach could possibly provide for its senior citizens without taxing everybody outrageously.

To the question "Why did you move?" the answers were surprisingly similar.

"There is so much for older people to do there! And we can always get into Laguna Beach in ten minutes if we want to come to the ocean—or shop."

At this writing the first tenants of Laguna Hills Leisure World are just beginning to move in. In order to find out how important these attractions had become to tenants and owners who have been residing in them a while we went to a number of retirement communities where residents had been living for several years.

A good part of the original euphoria induced by the pull of the *money magnets* still lingered. But, as might be expected, there was some disenchantment too.

In his book, *Let's Rejoin the Human Race,* Dr. Joseph H. Peck does a pretty thorough job of discouraging seniors from embracing the regimented life in these retirement communities. But Howard Whitman, in his book, *A Brighter Life,* seems to have found almost all of the elders enjoying their organized leisure as members of the "tended herd."

After scores of interviews, it would seem that most researchers are inclined to make a case for a personal point of view. The central purpose of this book is to let the retiree state his own case.

7

ON THE INSIDE LOOKING OUT

It is a temptation, when presenting material of this sort, to set it down in tidy "bookkeepers' columns" under such headings as THE CREDIT SIDE, THE DEBIT SIDE, and THE BALANCE. But to do this would be to do again what has already been done too often—to reduce warm, responsive, human beings to averages and statistics.

Obviously if one were going to record all of the pertinent quotes of all of the people interviewed it would be necessary to do one of two things, extend a book to encyclopedic length or convert reactions to mere tally marks in those columns.

We do not pretend that the individuals we have chosen to quote are average. We do not know what an average human being is—even if the insurance companies, the Bureau of Labor Statistics, the Census Bureau, and others appear to. If average means "ordinary" then certainly these retired seniors were far from average for we found extraordinary qualities in each. In everything they said we heard the clear ring of truth as they were discovering it in their reflections and experiences in retirement.

Mrs. Martha Williams is a seventy-year-old retired civil service employee. For several years she has lived alone in one of the great "city" type retirement complexes in Southern California.

When she retired in 1957 after more than thirty years in her job as a statistician she moved to Los Angeles to be nearer those cultural activities that stimulated her the most. But very soon Mrs. Williams had some second thoughts and moved back to the smaller community from which she had come.

When questioned about her decision she said, "Frankly, I couldn't take the smog!" But Mrs. Williams had another reason too:

"It was difficult to find reasonable living quarters. Before I chose this particular retirement community I tried several apartments, but transportation was always a problem. Then I looked into a number of those retirement hotels run by church groups.

"My goodness but they irritated me!" she exclaimed. "They are tax-free, you know, but they were the most expensive places I looked into. Why, one of them asked me to hand over fifteen thousand dollars for a little one-bedroom apartment. And on top of that they wanted to charge me fifty-six thousand dollars for meals and medical care for life."

Mrs. Williams shook her head in wonderment. "That would have come to over seventy thousand dollars, and I assure you that kind of money is just not available to a retired civil service employee."

Mrs. Williams conceded that if she had lived to be one hundred it might have been a "bargain" but she was also upset at the thought that should she die within a year or two the church group would have been able to keep all of the money paid in and would have had still another advantage: "They would have been able to clean up my apartment and sell it for full price all over again. And not only that," she added, "I just didn't like the idea of handing over all I've been able to accumulate and winding up with no estate left to give to my son and daughter-in-law."

In addition to her pension, which is modest but adequate for present needs, Mrs. Williams enjoys some benefits from her membership in the National Association for Retired People headquartered in Washington, D.C.

"But even with this insurance," she said, "I would be about five dollars a day short of what I would need for a double-occupancy room in our local hospital. Were I to be seriously ill for a long time all of the benefits would be used up and I'd be dipping into capital investments. I'm afraid I could not stand that for long. All of my life as a statistician I've been accustomed to facing facts," commented Mrs. Williams, "but I'm afraid that is one fact of retirement that I'm afraid to face. So, like most of us mortals, I guess I try not to think about such possibilities too much."

Mrs. Williams was asked if she *would* think about it—out loud—since most retirees confessed to the same fears.

"It is a nightmare," she replied. "This possibility of complete dependency upon one's children is a nightmare. Even with the most thoughtful, considerate children in the world it is a most dreadful prospect *for all of us.*"

Mrs. Williams did indicate that she had been able, during her married years, to build up a modest estate. "But it would not take much of an illness, really, to wipe out most everything we older people have managed to save. This is the most frightening prospect. A few years ago when medicine and hospitals were cheaper most of us might have squeaked through. But now there is no chance for most of us." And then she repeated, "Such a situation is the most dreadful prospect—*for all of us!*"

Before turning to some of the cheerful aspects of retirement, Mrs. Williams had more to say on the subject of illnesses.

"One thing we need here is a medical facility. They are talking about putting in a dispensary but mostly we have to call doctors from the outside or manage to get to the hospital in town. And another thing we need very badly is some sort of an alarm or signal system in case we get ill. I know they are putting them in the newer places now and I think it is a wonderful idea . . . very reassuring. If we had had some such arrangement here one of my neighbors could have been spared a terrible experience. She suffered a stroke and could not reach the telephone. She did manage to crawl outside on the lawn and was there some hours before a neighbor found her. Even if we'd had some sort of a patrol she would have been found sooner. It was a dreadful experience and I'm afraid it shook a number of us rather badly." Then, once again, Mrs. Williams repeated, "Illness is the most dreadful prospect—an ever-present fear—a nightmare!"

If the emphasis seems to be on fear it is because Mrs. Williams is voicing a universal fear—the dominant emotion of the aging retired. This fear increases with age. Quite often among the very old—the first-generation retired—we heard statements that went substantially like this: "Well—I'm so limited now—can't do things any more—I guess I'd be thankful if my time came any day now." But when the time approaches, those who do not go quickly suddenly rediscover the sweetness of life and cling to it with amazing tenacity.

This underlying fear increases with age. Quite apart from the inescapable fear of death that most of us must endure, under our present insurance and medical rates very little can be done by most people to dispel their fear of protracted illness and the dependency that usually accompanies it. "It is a nightmare for us all," says Mrs. Martha Williams, an alert, aware, articulate woman. And in so saying she reveals the carefully concealed central mechanism of The Retirement Trap.

Lest it seem that Mrs. Williams was preoccupied with the negative and the morbid, it should be said that by far the greater part of our visit with her was devoted to the more pleasant aspects of retirement. For the most part they are related to the social life.

One thing that strikes a visitor immediately is the preponderance of women in these retirement places. Though averages may be misleading they are unavoidable at times. Managers of the places visited confirmed that on the average women outnumber men by three to one.

Among these women, the elite are those who still have husbands to share their retirement. Among the male minority the most humorous and the most pathetic are the widowers. The most difficult men to get information from were the confirmed bachelors, who agreed with everything about everybody else but admitted nothing about themselves. They were also the most self-sufficient—or at least they put up the most convincing show. One gets the impression that they have insulated themselves against loneliness for so long that their bachelor way of life has indeed become for them a normal state. They are the least gregarious, staying pretty much to themselves, finding the greatest part of their social life "off the reservation" as one of them put it, except for their "foursomes" at golf. There is a definite feeling of defensiveness about this group and in the chapter called Cupid's Last Stand there is an explanation for this. But at this point the concern is primarily with *over-all inside impressions* of this new way of retirement.

So far as the husband and wife segment of the retirement society is concerned, no couple seemed more typical in their reactions than Mr. and Mrs. Elton Jones of Port St. Lucie in Martin County, Florida.

They were seated with friends on the veranda of the modest clubhouse overlooking the north fork of the St. Lucie River, some of the finest fishing waters in the world. Most of the small fishing boats were bobbing at their moorings though it seemed to be an ideal day. The conversation with the Jones couple grew out of our inquiries.

"We're not going to get much fishing in the north or south forks until we get some rain," said Mr. Jones. "We've had a long dry spell here. Rain puts oxygen in the water and then the fish get active again. They're down there all right—snook and bass—but they're not interested in any of the bait we've been dangling!"

Mr. and Mrs. Jones came from Phoenix, Arizona. When asked why they had not retired to the obvious place, Del Webb's Sun City right on the outskirts of town, Mrs. Jones answered, "Both Elton and I love the water. We're fishing nuts. When we knew that retirement was coming up we began making a series of trips in our car. We looked all over the country, the west coast, the east coast, up around New York, the west coast of Florida, but we finally settled here."

When asked about the summer heat in Phoenix, they replied, "No—the heat didn't bother us. We were used to it—and besides everything is air-conditioned anyway. Heat is no problem any more. Of course there is fishing in Lake Mead and Lake Mohave, but we wanted to live where we could have a choice of fresh- and salt-water fishing. Port St. Lucie is the most ideal place we found."

Mr. Jones added some pertinent information. "Apart from the fishing, we found that Port St. Lucie is best suited to our budget. Actually we could not afford to live in most of the other places. We figured it would have taken close to $7000 a year to live in Arizona or California. We live on considerably less than that here."

"And," Mrs. Jones interjected, "you can see that we live very comfortably."

They do indeed. Later, it was revealed that many persons in Port St. Lucie on the Atlantic coast and Port Charlotte on the Gulf coast lived on $3500 to $5000 a year. A few are said to be living solely on Social Security.

But none we met were free of the secret fear of protracted illness and its devastating expense. A man named Karl Mueller encountered at the bar in the golf club in another part of the same development put it more succinctly than anyone else:

"We are gambling that we are going to stay well until it's time to go—then go quick!"

Certainly it would not have been necessary to remind Mr. Mueller that the odds are overwhelmingly against such a gamble. Since the dawn of history man has been sustained by his belief. Generally he chooses to believe most passionately those ideas to which he can emotionally accommodate most comfortably. The cold, hard facts, if one can find them, are usually disconcerting.

The Joneses had more to say about their retired life at Port St. Lucie. When asked if they found time for any activities beyond their first love, fishing, Mrs. Jones indicated the activities calendar posted inside the clubhouse.

In seven days they had scheduled twenty different meetings of such groups as the fishing club, the bridge club, the poker club, the swimming club, the shuffleboard club, the sewing club, the square-dance class, and so on.

"Of course we don't get involved in them all," she explained, "but we do manage to take part in quite a few things."

Mr. Jones added the obvious. "A person can keep hopping around here if he has a mind to!"

A psychiatrist friend calls these retirees "the frantic funsters," a clever alliteration—and unfair. There are times while attending some of their dances and parties when one might be tempted to call them "the antic elders"—but without intent to deride. They are in a party mood and they are having fun. Some of the same men who cut up outlandishly at Shrine and American Legion conventions have belittled these elders for wearing "funny hats" or letting their hair down. There seemed to be no more of the "frantic" quality in these oldsters' "good times" than in those of any other group. And as for a great many of the conventioneers, one may well be a lot safer with the older cutups!

The figures available to most researchers, dealing in averages as they do, can be dangerously misleading if one takes them literally. For instance, it is said that there are two *generations* of retired persons included in the 18.7 million figure of those over sixty-five. That is true—so far as it goes. But one must not expect to divide them up handily into the sixty-five to eighty-five and the eighty-five to the centenarian groups.

Again, looking at people, not statistics, two generations were found to be living together in all of the retirement communities that did not require age sixty-five as the minimum for admittance.

The younger or "active retirement" generation ranged from fifty to seventy-five years of age. The older generation ranged from about seventy-five on up to include several nonagenarians

—one of whom worked a full week as linen mistress at the Army's remarkable Distaff House in Washington, D.C. Colonel V. W. Bond, the managing director, cited an example of this:

"Not long ago," he said, "I received a delegation of our older women who complained that 'those young whippersnappers [in their sixties and early seventies] were dominating the social life in the place.'"

The point is made in order to clarify the differences in needs and attitudes of the "young" elders and the "old" elders. Those interviewed so far may be said to belong squarely in the first group. Generally speaking they still have the time and energy to participate in the organized social life and recreational activity that is the wellspring of their happiness—pro tempore though it may be.

We disagree with the sociologists and gerontologists who seem to resent the fact that these seniors are not behaving in the theoretical manner. Again, statistics may enumerate and, to some extent, evaluate—but *the average man is a myth!* Why should these older people forsake pleasure, however frantic it may seem to these clinical observers? Why should they behave like graphs instead of grownups who know that a lot more of their years lie behind them than ahead and therefore are determined to "enjoy, enjoy" as Harry Golden puts it?

What if there is an element of determination in their fun-seeking? Is it foolish and graceless of them? And what about the truth in the statement of the old fellow on the golf course who said, "You younger people are gonna be downright surprised someday to find out just how precious a year can be when it might very well be your last one!" For too many of these so-called frantic funsters it will be!

This constant awareness of the imminence of death produces a number of problems for the administrators of the retirement homes and cities. In dozens of interviews we found management willing to discuss it "off the record" but few wished their particular retirement facilities to be identified.

When it came to securing permission for direct quotes most managers demurred.

Said one particularly able female administrator, "Death is around us in these places—in any place where there is a high concentration of elderly people. It poses some very difficult administrative and psychological problems."

When asked to illustrate with examples of these problems it became clear that for the administrator they are really one problem.

"I think all of our people are realists and willing to face the fact that after seventy time is growing short," she said. "But when death strikes a neighbor or a dear friend in these places it disrupts everyone badly."

We asked how management coped with the inevitable.

"By attending to the details as quickly and as quietly as possible. If death occurs in the hospital or in the nursing facility it is easier to handle. It is simpler to handle at night, too, when most of the residents are asleep. But not long ago we had one of our elderly ladies die in the social hall right after lunch. We went through a bad week with that one!"

We asked whether or not the effects of such deaths were greater in a retirement community than in any tightly knit suburban neighborhood.

"Yes," said the administrator, "primarily because in an average suburb you have a normal mixture of ages . . . age groups.

"I suspect that the older ones feel it more keenly than the younger ones who are shocked, of course, but who are so caught up in their vigorous daily pursuits that unpleasant emotions are soon displaced.

"In our retirement community even the youngest of our elders are not nearly so preoccupied with activities as they once were, and so it is natural that they'd be rather preoccupied with death. As a consequence they react more deeply when it strikes near them."

We asked what management might do to counteract these reactions.

"There are several things, yes. But they are somewhat above and beyond the call of duty. On our own time my staff and I do a great deal to get our elderly people interested in charitable work in the surrounding community. By that I mean *outside* of our own little retirement community. The games and the hobbies we provide are all right for a time. But I feel they just fill in time at best and that much more is accomplished by trying to *re-relate* our older ones to the greater community through some sort of charitable work."

This perceptive female administrator who has several such retirement communities to supervise indicated that this extroversion has been the most effective bulwark against the constant shock of the grim realities of life in its closing chapters. But only occasionally did we meet administrators whose duties permitted time for such extracurricular activities.

At Sacramento Manor, one of the three fine Boswell-Alliance retirement manors in the West, we talked more about the psychological aspects of supervising and administering a retirement community.

These unusual projects are private enterprise developments that carry their full share of the local, state, and federal tax burden. They appear to be among the best such profit-motivated retirement communities in the country. Their remarkably economical and efficient apartments and cottages are attractively planned in park-like surroundings and are within the reach of senior citizens in the lower-middle-income range. They are operated entirely on a monthly rental basis and the modest fees include the use of complete and well-planned recreational facilities.

Sacramento Manor is managed by H. D. Thomas, a retired civil engineer. To us he seemed to be one of the most aware and efficient managers in the country. Aided by Mrs. Thomas, he has quite justly earned the affection of the several hundred residents whose welfare he guards jealously.

It was obvious after visiting a great many retirement communities that just plain efficiency is not enough in a manager.

There must also be an awareness of the subtle techniques required in the handling of relationships with seniors. Mr. Thomas confirmed this.

"You cannot just sit down and make an arbitrary business decision in the usual way here," he said. "Decisions that affect the residents of a retirement community can have profound effects. There are very sensitive psychological problems involved here."

One aspect of the over-all problem was illuminated by Mr. Thomas: "When new residents come here there is a period of about six weeks when they are, you might say, lost. Then they begin to fasten on to new friends and they become dear friends very quickly. They have a great need for one another."

This observation had been fully confirmed by our own earlier research. In retirement communities, particularly in those that cater to the older segments of the retired group, it was not uncommon to see the most overt affection expressed at a chance meeting even though these same persons had encountered each other several times during the course of the day. Greetings are marked by embraces among the women and there is much "cheek-pecking" upon departures and rather more use of endearments than one would probably have found among the same group of ladies a decade or so earlier when they were still occupied with family routine.

When asked about this, one of the most articulate of the ladies in a Pennsylvania retirement community replied, "I suppose we are so 'affectionate' as you call it because for the first time in our lives we have time to reflect upon just how dear friendships can be. So many of us have been selfish during our busy years and we have brushed aside many relationships that might have been warm and wonderful. Perhaps," she said pointedly, "we're trying to make up for our selfishness now."

When asked to evaluate this point of view the great majority of older women agreed willingly to its validity. But only a small minority would attribute any part of their need for affection to the fact that they have found themselves isolated from their families to an extent far greater than they had anticipated. They refused to acknowledge it even after they had freely confessed, even complained, that in retirement they do not see members of the family as often as they did previously.

In the best of the retirement communities, particularly the smaller ones limited to several hundred residents, we found management most aware of the senior's special needs. We found administrators taking pains to make their older people feel wanted and needed. One result is that staff members often find that residents transfer affections to them together with problems and decisions. Duties devolve upon management that should be undertaken by the grown children of these older ones—the same children who in so many cases—*far too many cases*—actually do consider these places "dumping grounds," although they would protest righteously and rationalize outrageously if ever confronted with their own selfishness.

One cannot escape the impression that in a great number of instances the older ones are far better off in the considerate and comfortable atmosphere of the best of these retirement communities than they would be if left to their own devices in the old family place from which the younger generations have departed. Certainly this is true in the cases of those who must spend their final years getting by on extremely modest incomes and therefore cannot find solace in trips abroad or in frequent visits to understanding but expensive family doctors.

But it is important to make the distinction between the "younger" and the "older" oldsters. The problems touched on undoubtedly are accentuated as the younger ones become the older ones. Modern retirement communities have not been in operation long enough to provide us with an accurate continuing picture of this physical and emotional transition and its special needs. But there can be little doubt that adjustments will become increasingly difficult as advancing age limits those physical and social activities that tend to produce this merciful state of near euphoria.

The question that needs answering is, what happens when a long-time resident of one of these places finally comes to realize that he or she can no longer take part in the diversions that produced a feeling of happiness and well-being? What will be the psychological impact and the physiological effect of this sudden realization that one is no longer *needed* in that younger, more active segment of the retirement society?

Perhaps part of the answer may be found in the statement made by an old gentleman in the lobby of the Roosevelt Hotel, now a retirement hotel, in Washington, D.C. He wore a look of wistful resignation.

"Can I tell you the truth?" he said. "When you are young you got three, maybe four close friends. You got no time for more. But when you get old, like me, you need anyway *ten* close friends—with the same problems you got!"

This point of view seemed to agree with that of H. D. Thomas at Sacramento Manor, three thousand miles to the west.

"They begin to fasten on to new friends and they become dear friends very quickly. They have a great *need* for one another. . . ."

Always, the key word is *need*.

But whatever their shortcomings—and as residents grow older these shortcomings increase—the best of these new retirement communities offer an effective solution to at least part of the emotional needs of the retiree. As they are presently conceived, these places are most effective for the residents who are still in their active retirement years.

It does not seem likely that any of these places will ever be able to offer more than a partial solution to the problems of the aging. After all, the only real alternative to death is immortality. So far not even the most extravagant promotion men have dared hold out that hope. On the contrary, at least one place in Southern California and one in Arizona are located within easy pall-bearing distance of spacious new cemeteries. One new retirement village called Friendly Valley is actually adjacent to a new cemetery called Eternal Valley.

As one resident said, "It's handy all right—if you don't think about it too much!"

With its lavishly appointed recreational facilities including everything from tiddly-winks to tournament golf, it would seem that the management of Friendly Valley is doing everything it can to keep residents from thinking about anything too much—at least during their waking hours.

8

THE SWINGING SAMARITANS

We are absolutely convinced that if Lawrence Welk were to announce his candidacy the senior citizens would elect him President of the United States by an overwhelming majority. Guy Lombardo would probably be vice-president.

Of all the activities in these retirement communities, dancing seems to be the most popular.

As one manager put it, "These Olympic-sized swimming pools are nothing but sales hooks and status symbols. You've got to have them or they think you're a second-rate place. But the one facility that really gets a workout is the community hall, where the dances are held."

We attended a dozen such functions and each one was a sellout. Most often the dancing was done to hi-fi. But quite frequently small orchestras or combos are engaged to play at the big weekend dances.

Second only to Lawrence Welk in popularity are the country and western groups and the polka groups. Welk and Lombardo —and Wayne King, too—are universally accepted. They seem to have no special regional appeal.

Western square-dance music is extremely popular. The polka groups seem to find their greatest acceptance around the Great Lakes. Any man who can call a square dance is automatically a celebrity as is any man or woman who can play an instrument. The Harry Truman school of piano playing predominates. But here and there one finds a real old-fashioned "ivory tickler," the sort known in Dad's youth as a high-class "H-house" piano player. When these seniors perform, the password is *one more time!"*

There is nothing frantic about this dancing. The oldsters move through the disciplines of the square dance with zest but always with great dignity. An observer would be remiss if he did not pay a special compliment to their appearance. The women often have as many as a half-dozen square-dance dresses, usually self-designed and made.

At Art Linkletter's Sierra Dawn retirement community in Hemet, California, one of the female employees in the recreation center said, "Before a special dance party you almost have to wait in line to get into the sewing room!"

None of the special dance dresses are costly. They are made up of ginghams and other inexpensive cottons that "move" well. To see a roomful of older women, their graying hair all carefully set, whirling with their courtly partners decked out in western clothes and dancing boots, is a very special and appealing experience. If one observes with half-closed eyes, a sort of magic takes place and years seem to fade away. This same magic works on both participant and spectator. "We have never danced as much as we have here," was a typical response. This was confirmed by several couples who supplement their income by teaching square dancing, the reels, and the polka. In effect, they said:

"Most of these folks danced quite a bit when they were young. But they got out of the habit. Now they are learning all over again and enjoying it more than ever."

But "after the ball is over, after the break of morn," the magic time reverser ceases its work and the older ones are back in the present again, with all of its problems.

At all of the recreation centers it is in these meeting rooms, card rooms, and billiard rooms that retirees find most of the diversions that provide a pleasant anesthesia.

Next to dancing, card games seem to be the most popular

indoor group activity. At one evening of cards at Del Webb's Kern City there were forty-four tables of bridge. At some of the places gin rummy was played in the afternoon. In fact, in Florida it seemed to be the preferred game.

At most of the retirement communities the men managed to appropriate a room for themselves. These "Men Only" retreats are variously named but the most popular label seems to be "the Dog House." They grow out of a fundamental need.

Spike Bentley, a retired construction executive with a talent for terse observations put it this way:

"For most wives retirement means a lot less money and a lot more husband. Perhaps a woman doesn't feel so strongly about having her man underfoot as he feels guilty about being there."

If there seemed to be a certain amount of self-conscious flippancy in the men's attitude toward being underfoot in their new position as one of the retired there was certainly none in the attitude of most of the women.

Not all of them understood the nature of the psychological problem retirement had created for their husbands. But here and there we met thoughtful women who had anticipated the problems that might arise.

Mrs. Clarence Fortman of Kansas City was one such. She and her husband had been able to take comfortable surroundings in one of the smaller retirement communities near Galveston where one of their sons and his family had settled.

"No matter how well you know your man," said Mrs. Fortman, "I do not think it is possible to anticipate all of the problems. But it certainly helps if you understand something about the basic problem. In the two years that Clarence has been retired I have had a chance to watch others in the same condition. The greatest problem to combat is a feeling of uselessness. These men feel more like unemployed persons than retired ones who have earned their leisure. They feel there is little dignity in their status and they resent it deeply and that resentment comes out in little ways that can be trying to a wife who doesn't understand."

When asked what she thought to be the predominant emotion in her husband and in his contemporaries Mrs. Fortman answered:

"Guilt, I'd say. I know it sounds ridiculous . . . but there's little reason in emotion. I think they feel less guilty about loafing as retirement wears on. But if they've been responsible men . . . they feel some guilt. They would deny it hotly. But they feel it!"

No unanimity of professional opinion about this aspect of The Retirement Trap was found among gerontologists and sociologists. In fact, there is almost no agreement among these people on any aspect of the problems of aging except that too little is known about them.

Dr. Donald Kent, Director of the Office of Aging in the Department of Health, Education and Welfare in Washington, D.C., said, "One of the great problems lies in the fact that the *quality of age* is not valued in our society. This results in the aged not valuing themselves." Then, with unusual candor, Dr. Kent added, "Those of us who are trying to cope with the problem intelligently are limited by our insight. There is a vast difference between theory and experience. In some instances it seems to be mainly a matter of theory *versus* experience."

To illustrate this point Dr. Kent told of a call from an eminent professor of gerontology at a midwestern university. "I've called you," said the savant, "to warn you not to put too much faith in my last book on the subject. Since it has been published I have gathered evidence through research that would seem to indicate that some of my former theories were wrong!"

Under Dr. Kent's section in Washington a great deal of experience is being accumulated. From it will undoubtedly emerge some enlightened new theories about the nature and the handling of the problems of aging, the problems of integrating into our total society that once-prized segment of productive contributors for whom there is no longer a place at present.

How do retirees themselves feel about their displacement? Once again a most succinct and accurate answer from Spike Bentley:

"Futility is the retired man's biggest battle. He says, 'What am I going to do today? And what difference does it make anyway?'"

At Kern City, William Moran, a retired accountant for the U. S. Geological Survey, puts it this way:

"The worst thing that can happen to you is to become a ho-hummer."

When asked to define one, he replied, "You know, one of those fellows who gets up in the morning and says, 'Ho-hum, what am I going to do today?'"

Like Mr. Bentley, Mr. Moran has ample opportunity to work part-time in his former profession if he cares to. But Bill Moran has an absorbing hobby. He is a model-railroad expert. And the layout he showed us with justifiable pride was not only an engineering marvel—all built by hand—but an artistic creation as well. In addition, Bill Moran would qualify as a first-rate barrel-house pianist and therefore is in great demand at social functions.

Bill's wife, Mrs. Ethel Moran, is a retired schoolteacher. With two retirement incomes the Morans are somewhat better fixed than most. In such circumstances—and in these large retirement communities there are many residents who may be called well-off—some couples seek their diversions in travel rather than in activities related to the social and recreation facilities, most of which are administered by resident committees.

But Mr. and Mrs. Moran know that in retirement living it is especially true that one receives in proportion to his giving. And so they give generously of their time and energy and help to organize many of the social functions that liven up this way of life.

Mrs. Moran often writes for the little newspaper that is circulated around Kern City. When asked for her impression of life at the community she quoted from an essay on retirement living that she had read before a town assembly.

Excerpts from it comprise a revealing distillation of the essence of the spirit in all of these large retirement communities in every part of the country. Implied is the essential sameness of the problem and the need.

Wrote Mrs. Moran, *"There is a definite feeling of belonging . . . we are caught up in a surge of friendliness from all sides . . . a feeling that we want to help one another. . . ."* Again, the need to be needed.

Perhaps those who deride the liveliness with which these newly retired people undertake their social activities do so because they instinctively understand but fear to acknowledge the inevitableness of these needs. Derision is certainly one manifestation of fear. The fear of death is inherent in all men. It runs like a dark thread through man's mythology from the beginning of recorded experience.

The surge of "friendliness," as Mrs. Moran describes it, was evident at every retirement community visited. When asked to explain this phenomenon, sociologists were divided. The explanations varied and did not satisfy: "You must consider that these places are like clubs. They attract a segment of society that is more gregarious—usually people from smaller towns—joiners, you might call them. . . ." Or, "In fact, most of these people are like kids in a toy shop before Christmas. They have never been able to afford all of the recreation facilities they now find for a pittance at places like Leisure World or Sun City. They are excited—the novelty hasn't worn off—they want to show off their new toys—they want to make certain everybody who comes into their lives is aware of their new affluence."

It did not seem true, however, that only small-town joiners gravitated to such retirement communities. On the contrary a preponderance of seniors came from cities and crowded suburbs. Most of them had not belonged to country clubs or yacht clubs. The women seemed to have taken part in the normal community activities—P.T.A., Brownies, a bridge club, a garden club. But many of them said they had been too busy raising families to do more than engage in a little church activity.

The men—and they ranged from an ambassador, a brigadier general, and a former state senator to the owner of a franchised ice-cream stand, the manager of a dry-cleaning plant, and a retired plumber—belonged to professional clubs, associations, and unions. Only one, the former ambassador, had once belonged to a golf club in Maryland.

Their incomes had ranged from $10,000 to over $25,000 a year. They were not men who would normally have become close friends in their former societies. And still these retirees, all deliberately chosen from one retirement city, had become good friends. They served on recreational committees and played golf together. The owner of the ice-cream stand and the former ambassador were both lawn-bowling champions and officials of the intercity league. In their contacts with outsiders and with their fellow retirees, these men and their wives (who had also become close friends) were outgoing in the same degree. There was no apparent reserve. Neither was there any obvious self-consciousness or overheartiness in their manners. As Mrs. H. Bentley put it, "Most of these people are just plain friendly."

But is it really "plain" friendliness? There seemed to be one obvious quality that set this friendliness apart from what might commonly be called the *average* tenor of relationships between friends and acquaintances. The quality was a concern compounded of consideration and thoughtfulness—not a dominant quality in the commercial and professional fields that comprise our highly competitive society.

Hundreds of interviews in scores of retirement establishments reduce to but a tiny fraction of the total condition. And still, just as it is possible to determine the major characteristics of sea water from an analysis of a single drop, so it may also be possible to determine the characteristics of this new society of retirees from these relatively small examples.

As with drops of water from different oceans, there may be a trace more salinity in one. There was a trace more taciturnity in New England than in Florida and a trace more vigor in Texas than in Oregon. But the essential qualities were the same.

Though the psychologists and sociologists have undoubtedly touched on elements of the truth in their necessarily superficial studies of these communities (they are too new to provide long-term observations) it seemed that the really significant behavior difference lies in the quality of *concerned consideration* already noted.

Even allowing for the fact that retirees in any given type of community are "in the same boat" in many respects, that would not seem to be a sufficient problem-in-common to cause a marked effect on their behavior.

The cause may lie far deeper. It may lie in a new need that, for all its apparent unselfishness, is in fact a form of selfishness. In the relentless competition of the open market place, single-minded selfishness is one of man's most effective weapons. The requirements of the battle provide their own rationalization for such behavior. Church, lodge, and other "good works" provide a psychological buffer that permits a self-centered man to prevail on the battlefield.

But when the years of daily battles are over and it becomes apparent that in the end all of the combatants are destined to lose the war, there may be an urgent individual need to expiate those old crimes of selfishness in overt acts of *unselfish concern* for one's fellow survivors. . . . Paradoxically, this need itself may be the *ultimate selfishness*—a form of subconscious account-squaring before Judgment Day.

We have observed this closely among the elderly of both sexes in our own large family and in the families of our friends. We saw no significant difference between their behavior and the behavior of their contemporaries in the retirement communities.

No criticism is implied. The selfish need is self-mitigating. The joy of such dedicated service to new friends may be a subtle form of self-conferred absolution.

Mrs. Ruth Woolen of Kern City may have said it all in this admonition:

"When you retire, find something you can do for somebody else. If you don't, you are going to die!"

9

THE NOT-SO-LIVELY ARTS?

Next in sales importance to the Olympic-sized swimming pools and the king-sized community centers are the buildings in which the hobby rooms are housed. In many ways they are the most subtle *money magnets* of all for they appeal very strongly to those persistent but inconsistent good intentions that pave purgatory.

If there was one universal quote among the ladies it was this:

"I've never had time for a hobby. But I'm going to take one up just as soon as . . . we get settled—our children leave for home—Fred is feeling better again," and so on, ad infinitum.

Strangely enough there was no such universal quote from the men so far as the hobbies were concerned.

Standard equipment for this aspect of retirement living is a sewing room, a wood-working room, a lapidary room for rock-hounds, a photo studio, a painting and sculpture studio, and a ceramic studio. But inquiries into what is commonly held to be the busiest of all these facilities disclosed that in most of the places these *money magnets* produced little more than the original exclamations of delight prior to the handing over of the down payment.

The most active hobby rooms were in those retirement communities where instructors were provided without additional charge. The busiest of all hobby rooms, regardless of charges, were the sewing rooms. And surprisingly enough a number of men were at work in them! Discreet questioning revealed the fact that all of them were retired tailors. One man was making himself a beautiful Harris tweed suit from material his daughter purchased in Scotland during a vacation trip. Another man, a former ladies' tailor from Chicago, was making a handsome suit for one of the women who lived nearby.

When we exclaimed with genuine admiration at his craftsmanship, he looked over his glasses a bit sadly and said, "Sitting here with all these gabby women ain't like it was in my own shop but I make a nice dollar this way—when I feel like it." He finished basting a sleeve, then added, "I have to charge the same as outside. If I start making bargains, I'll be working eighteen hours a day!"

Classes in drawing, oil painting, and water coloring were not large in any of the places. Management did not admit this. But the reason was disclosed by some of the ladies.

"If you have a limited income you just cannot afford to get involved in too many of these hobbies. I contribute fifty cents a lesson toward the painting teacher. For a while we had a free teacher from the adult education staff of the local school district. But the teacher taught us like we were children and after a while we got bored. We got rid of him. Some of us may be in our second childhood but we don't want to be taught like first graders!"

Another lady said, "By the time you buy your paints and your canvas and all of the things you need you have spent fifty dollars just to get started. I thought I wanted to do it but when I found out how much it was costing me to ruin a canvas every week I gave up painting for ceramics. I don't do much better, artistically, but at least when I ruin an ash tray it only costs a few hours and a few cents."

There were some people using the photo laboratories. Most often they were the public relations men developing press shots. In one studio a professional photographer had set up shop and traded instruction for space and the use of the community equipment. He is kept busy.

The wood-working shops seemed moderately busy. Few men were actually at work but sawdust and shavings were in evidence—sure signs that former "slaw" students were trying their hands at footstools again.

There seems to be a small but dedicated group of rockhounds in most of the western retirement communities. The diamond saws and polishers and tumblers get a good workout after each field trip. There is a lot of beauty locked in the slabbed stones. Somehow though it seems that a rather small percentage of it ever survives the design and execution and reaches the finished rings, bracelets, and bolas. There are exceptions. A few of the pieces are being made by men and women hobbyists who have become expert gem cutters. Their work is extraordinarily beautiful.

Occasionally these hobbies turn into rewarding professions and form the basis for a whole new career. Such is the case with Russ Hind of Laguna Beach, California. After many years as a successful building contractor, Russ decided to take it easy. He and his lovely wife, Esther, retired to a trailer park overlooking the Pacific and began pursuing their long-time hobby of rock-hounding.

Their talent for turning agate, turquoise, opal, jade, and other stones into exquisitely designed jewelry led to such a demand that they opened a modest shop on South Coast Highway.

In time they were prevailed upon to exhibit some of their jewelry in the famous Laguna Beach Festival of Arts. And now, many first and second prizes later, Russ Hind's name engraved on a piece of handmade jewelry is equivalent to the name Tiffany on more pretentious jewels.

Frequently, Russ and Esther Hind retire from their second full-time careers by locking up for weeks at a stretch while they explore remote desert and mountain areas all over the West in search of exciting new raw materials.

Their story is cited here because, for those entering their retirement years, the Hinds' experience contains a message of hope. If one is willing to make the effort—and assuming a modicum of aptitude—this sort of active retirement can be one of life's rewarding experiences. Personally—and without making any special attempt to find them—we came across a dozen retired persons who have turned an aptitude into a hobby and then gone on to develop that hobby into a doubly rewarding second career.

One is a ceramist who specializes in mosaic tabletops. They are works of art and very costly, but nonetheless she has orders enough to keep her busy for a full year—and has had such orders for several years now. Her work is her own best advertisement and it is not unusual for her to receive orders sight unseen from persons in faraway states.

Another has turned his wood-carving hobby into a profitable retirement profession. He makes custom-carved panels in standard sizes. Fine furniture makers incorporate them in showpieces and sell them at premium prices. Recently he did the panels for two huge church doors. The task took six months and earned him $5000.

Still another retired woman has learned the difficult art of starting miniature trees much like the Japanese bonzai trees. In collaboration with a ceramist she does special work for architects and interior decorators. Her added income amounts to several thousand dollars a year. In this woman's case she is investing the money in carefully selected stocks and bonds to be used to cover unusual medical expense if and when approaching old age brings long illnesses that might otherwise deplete her estate.

These persons are in the minority, of course. But their activities do point a way out of The Retirement Trap for far more talented and dexterous persons than are presently engaged in hobby activities.

These pursuits depend largely upon temperament, of course. There is an old saying in the Army that no man ever became a good general unless he had once been a good second lieutenant. There is a much newer saying in the retirement communities to the effect that a person who was lazy during the earlier years will be lazy during the retirement years.

How often women have been heard to say, "But I'm not equipped to do anything. I've been a housewife and mother all of my life. The only thing that I ever did was take part in a little club work after the children had grown up."

They tended to ignore completely the fact that a skilled housewife is one of the most efficient and versatile workers in the world's economy. But these imagined limitations need not inhibit an aware and determined woman, as the story of a lady we will call Louise Cowles will demonstrate.

Mrs. Cowles, approaching her retirement years, simply refused to go to seed. During the family-raising years she had been moderately active in club work. When she was left alone she organized a new concept in book and authors clubs in her community. Several times a year Mrs. Cowles would arrange luncheons. Authors whose current works were on the best-seller lists would be guest speakers. From the beginning the affairs were successfully run because Mrs. Cowles had applied her housewifely organization to the problem and had chosen her speakers with great care.

After several years it became clear that there was an urgent need for someone who understood authors and their problems and could do, on a personal basis, the sort of promotion that a publisher can seldom do. Though Mrs. Cowles had not worked before and had no economic need to, she began to think of ways and means to widen the reputations of deserving writers.

Very soon grateful authors were singing her praises, and in a surprisingly short time the executive editorial staff of a book publishing company heard about her work.

At first Mrs. Cowles was uncertain about taking a position with anybody. Finally, when the means to accomplish her objectives were promised, she accepted on a part-time basis.

Working alone on a limited experimental budget, Louise Cowles began lining up radio, television, and club appearances for her authors. Almost overnight she had become the leading authors' promotional representative in her region.

We know many women who have retired much younger than Louise Cowles. They seem decades older, physically and mentally.

"If you give in and let your interest in people lag," she warns, "you will start going to seed the day you retire!"

There was no mistaking her determination when she concluded her observations by saying, "I have no intention of slowing down. Once you make up your mind to do that it is only a matter of a very short time until you are slowed to a stop!"

An increasing number of doctors and gerontologists are coming around to that point of view. There was a time not long ago when most doctors felt that an older person who made that sort of statement was courting sudden death. But no longer. Most physicians feel now that such resolution tempered with a little common sense may add significantly to one's useful years.

Several of the larger retirement communities are now considering not only furnishing expert instructors in the most popular hobbies but they are trying to find ways, within reason, to include the cost of raw materials in the over-all recreation charge that is a part of most of these retirement plans.

If they can make the economics work, they feel that much new enjoyment and meaning can be given to the active retirement years—and that the active years may be appreciably extended.

"Most of us are not self-starters any more," said Mrs. Amy Freed, formerly of Miami and now living at Sacramento Manor. She pointed to the very attractive summer dress she was wearing. "Would you believe it? I made this dress. I made it in the sewing room here—and I have never sewed a stitch in my life. That is the honest truth!"

When asked what stimulated her interest, she replied, "A new friend here at the Manor. I was going to buy a light dress and she said, 'Why don't you make one yourself?'"

Mrs. Freed chuckled. "The idea scared me to death! But my friend took me shopping, we picked out some material and a pattern, and the next thing I knew I was in the sewing room basting away just like I knew what I was doing."

It was obvious that Mrs. Freed had soon learned what she was doing—and in learning she had opened the door to a stimulating new experience.

"Now that I got lucky with this first dress I'm going to try some more," she confided. "My son and daughter-in-law still don't believe it. Me sewing!"

Her laugh is wonderful. So is her spirit.

10

YOU CAN TAKE IT WITH YOU, BUT IT PROBABLY WON'T FIT!

In most of the retirement communities there was only one area in which there were apparent attempts to create misleading impressions. That was in the decoration of the model apartments and in some of the smaller single dwellings.

These overdecorated models are usually the most effective sales motivators. Even in the least expensive communities, comparative fortunes had been spent on creating the twin illusions of opulence and spaciousness.

The techniques are subtle and effective—another sort of subliminal salesmanship that launches a many-pronged attack on the senses and cleverly directs the resulting reactions into a "buy now" frame of mind.

Color is used profusely and generally in excellent taste. Texture is used to the n-th degree in upholstering, in carpeting, and in paneling. And sound is used. Stereo-hi-fi fills the rooms of all of the models with the muted, whipped-cream arrangements of Andre Kostelanetz and David Rose, the sugary, corn-ball concertos of Liberace and the titillating rinkey-tink of Welkian waltzes. Once in a while someone smuggles in a good Roger Williams album.

But the greatest ingenuity of all is used in furnishing the really modest space offered in most of these "popularly priced" places.

Those developments that offer full-sized houses, separate dwellings such as one might find in any suburban tract, have less need for camouflaging their limitations in square footage. Consequently, in them, furniture compared favorably in size with the conventional pieces that one usually finds in the average family home.

But in those condominiums and cooperatives—in the apartment concept of dwelling which is favored by many of the retirement communities—it was often another story.

In many of the floor plans, *usable, enclosed living space* seldom exceeded 750 square feet. But in this area the architects had sometimes managed to parcel up as much as a living room, a dining alcove, a spacious kitchen, two bedrooms, and two baths. In many cases the square footage was advertised as being well over a thousand. But this was weasel-wording to include small atriums or covered (but not enclosed) patios. "Two baths" often turned out to be only a bath and a half. One ingenious space-saving design combines two adjacent toilets and basins with a combination tub and shower between them.

How then do the decorators manage to create the illusion of space in these really small places? *They use scaled-down furniture* and *mirrors*.

Very few of the prospective buyers who wander through these lavishly furnished layouts in a state of semienchantment have either the vision or the desire to mentally substitute their own generously sized Grand Rapids, Early American, or overstuffed furniture for the sleek Danish modern, the fragile French "Louis" reproductions, or the "new version" Spanish suites that are chosen and positioned so cleverly.

Sofas and sectionals often are the smallest stock pieces to be had. Quite often they are upholstered in fabrics that utilize the same principle as Mother Nature's protective coloration on her wild creatures—they are made to blend into wall-to-wall carpeting and into wallpaper or paneling. On a smoggy day it would have been difficult to see some of them without the cerise, aquamarine, and shocking-pink pillows used to accentuate them.

Ottomans are liberally deployed in odd corners as are fragile-looking contemporary chairs, occasional pieces, and small tables. Most of the chairs are so low that even a spry senior citizen would have great difficulty in lowering himself onto one of them, much less rising again.

Windows are decorated with valances and swags that cost hundreds of dollars for just the living room alone. Some of the bedrooms are wreathed in clouds of dotted swiss and organdy or are hung with formal brocades and velours that cost upward of twenty dollars a yard.

The conservative walls seldom have more than one fair-sized painting. But most often there are clusters of arty-smarty little doodads, phony coins in shadow boxes, phony keys on phony marble plaques, phony African masks, phony antique candleholders, sconces, and the like.

The rooms are awash in a sea of gimcracks, knick-knacks, and "precious" little decorators' items that are as ridiculous as the price tags concealed on their backsides.

In one Southern California retirement development the salesman was disarmingly candid:

"These furnished models are the 'closers' for us. We take people through all of the recreation and hobby stuff first, then we turn them loose alone in these apartments. If they are serious prospects, they come out sold! That is why we give our decorators a blank check."

In another large development in the same general price range in the San Francisco area a young decorator was discovered at work in a partially completed model apartment. When asked if he thought any of the buyers would actually furnish their places so lavishly he threw up his hands in dismay.

"Good grief, no!" he exclaimed. "We simply *load* these places!"

To find out just what was meant by "loading," a professional decorator friend was asked to visit a few of the model homes at retirement communities in the West. Her findings were a revelation.

In the model apartments that sold for under $20,000, the furnishings did not vary in total by more than 10 per cent from one project to another. And in no case did the retail price of the sample furnishings total less than two thirds of the sales price of the empty apartment. In one unit that was priced just under $18,000 the carpeting, drapes, furniture, and knick-knacks that had been loaded into it computed, at retail, totaled $18,557.50! One wall was stacked floor to ceiling with eight coordinated, oiled-walnut, Danish modern bookcases and cabinets. The price was $2400. There were two hand-woven area rugs over the basic carpeting. The decorator said she had just purchased two like it from the same weavers in Long Island, New York. One cost $600 and the other $800.

Two Mexican primitive wood carvings of religious figures, each about eighteen inches tall, had cost $400. An original oil painting carried a $1200 price tag discreetly concealed on the back of the frame. The painting by a brilliant young California artist was very interesting. But it was hardly the sort that a senior citizen would be likely to prefer to a fine Robert Wood landscape or a good print of Rosa Bonheur's "The Horse Fair." But it did its part to create an atmosphere of contemporary opulence and sophistication.

Of course the old stand-by, mirrors, did much to increase the apparent size of the rooms too. In the living room, antique gold mirror covered one entire wall—over $500 worth. And in the bedroom, a scaled-down canopied bed reflected its flounced and spindly elegance against a solid wall of plate glass mirror that cost over $300.

A steel tape measure proved to be a revealing tool. In several model retirement homes, the decorators had used children's beds under six feet in length to create the illusion of spaciousness in many of the small, second bedrooms. After pointing this out to a sales representative, he admitted that they were indeed children's beds—put there on purpose.

"You see," he explained, "we feel that in these active retirement communities we should make provisions for children." Then he added hastily, *"Grandchildren,* of course—they are welcome to visit here anytime!"

Management may welcome them all right—under certain very stringent rules—but some of the older grandparents do not.

"I can take my own son and daughter for about half a day," said one lady. "And I can take my grandchildren for about half an hour."

This lady and a number of other seniors—both men and women—had the same reservations about unrestricted visits from the "Bang! Bang! You're dead!" set.

"I love them with all my heart," she added, "but they do wear me down and there is nothing for them to do here, so they get restless. You see they are not allowed in the pool or on the shuffleboard courts."

In several communities there are facilities for entertaining the little nippers. But in most retirement places grandmother and grandfather, for all of their love, are under a strain if the grandchildren come too frequently and stay too long.

One thing that strikes a visitor to these retirement dwellings is the almost universal presence of what appears to be old family china and glassware.

"Our silver plate and glassware and dishes are about the only things that would fit," said one woman. "And even then we thinned the sets down to a service for six. The rest of it is in storage because we have no room for it here."

Another woman said, "At first we planned to bring most of our things from the old house. But when we did some measuring we found that very little of it would fit without crowding everything together. We still have a lot of things in storage and it is costing us about twenty dollars a month. Sooner or later

I guess we'll get up courage enough to dispose of them. We need that money for other things now."

Mrs. Amy Freed at Sacramento Manor had another idea. "I came here without a knife and fork—furnished everything from scratch. I don't see any sense in paying room rent or storage for furniture I can't use. I had a fourteen-room house and I tell you I wouldn't go through that responsibility again for anything!"

With very few exceptions it was the couples who were still together who seemed to feel the need for some sort of continuity—some material tie with the past. This also seemed true of maiden ladies who had lived alone most of their lives.

Widows and widowers tended to go to extremes. Either they wanted all of the old things around them—or practically none. This latter attitude was the prevalent one.

Of course there are always some special little mementos that had great significance—books, pictures, a vase. Beds in which there had been long illnesses or deaths were left behind in favor of new ones, not associated with unhappy memories. Dead husbands' favorite chairs were left behind, usually given to grown children. Most of the widows had lived for some time in the midst of the old familiar things. By the time they moved to a retirement community they were ready for a break with the past—usually at the urging of their children.

It is obvious that the majority of retirees do attempt to bring too many of the old furnishings with them. Two situations usually result: a packing and shipping charge that takes a big bite out of newly reduced budgets and an anachronous furnishing job that clashes with the slick modern design and materials of the new living space. Quite apart from the fact that the old stuff doesn't look right in its new setting, there just plain isn't room enough for most of it. Often another unscheduled expense results when smaller new pieces are substituted for old.

Most of the retirees come from spacious living quarters that belong to another era. True the old houses may have been a bit short of bathrooms. But usually there were plenty of other rooms in which to rear a family and in most cases there was an attic or a basement to accommodate the surplus things that were no longer needed but were "too good to throw away."

In the cases where people had made a clean break with the past and had started with bare walls, the majority had purchased new furniture on time. Some of it was good but most of it was flashy or flimsy or both and would probably deteriorate long before the final installment payment.

"When we bought this stuff," groaned one discouraged husband, "we were told it was the same sort of furniture we had seen in the model apartment. Maybe so, but it doesn't look the same in here."

Of course not! All of the professional decorating tricks were missing. Also the decorators use only the finest quality furniture in the sales models.

As stated earlier, the retirement community concept is still too new to have provided any broad body of research from which completely dependable conclusions may be drawn. But there is some evidence that the problem of what to keep and what to discard when one changes to this new mode of living is both puzzling and costly.

Ross Cortese recognized that such a problem existed. And he recognized a profitable promotional device. When Leisure World No. 2 was planned at Laguna Hills, California, and No. 3 at Walnut Creek, across the bay from San Francisco, Mr. Cortese provided for furniture stores on the premises. Just off the lobbies of the sales offices one now finds elegant new display rooms where residents may buy excellent merchandise at competitive prices.

Most of the furniture is made by nationally known manufacturers and while it might be possible to save a few dollars on the same pieces by watching department-store sales, the convenience of having the Leisure World stores right in one's front yard and the savings in time make the idea sensible. Consequently the stores do very well.

An official of the Public Relations Division of the New York City Housing Authority pointed out a growing racket among unscrupulous furniture dealers.

Using the innocuous time-payment plan, many of these "vultures," as this official correctly termed them, persuade retired persons *in the low-income brackets* to "trade in" valuable old furniture that has served for years for smaller, scaled-down pieces of decorative apartment-sized junk that will become shabby and useless within two or three years, at which time another devastating expense faces the oldster.

"The elderly are the new victims of these despicable furniture merchants," said the official with great feeling. "Of course the vultures victimize younger persons too. But the young ones have not given up fine old pieces for junk. And more important still, the young couples have years of earning power ahead of them. They can afford a few mistakes. These older, retired people cannot."

Perhaps someday the best developers will have paid consultants available to residents of their great new retirement communities, experts who can sit down and counsel with the newcomer, go over a list of their old furniture and from it select certain pieces that will work well in the new quarters. These pieces could then be complemented by new ones and by proper carpeting and drapes. Or old pieces could be refinished, recovered, or slip-covered to tie in with a new theme of decor. In this manner, much fine furniture could be saved and made to work happily with the new. But even more important, precious retirement dollars could be saved. Or perhaps some enterprising decorators will see the possibilities and advertise such a service for retirees at a reasonable fee.

Most people in modest circumstances have little contact with good, professional interior decorators. From time to time they may get a suggestion or two from one of the consultants who work in the furniture departments of the larger department stores. But generally these pointers would have to do with minor problems, not with the over-all decorating scheme.

Several hours of consultation on the problem of decorating a new home would and should cost the prospective buyer a few dollars. But it would be money well spent and might do much to stop a remark heard time and time again:

"It doesn't look much like the furnished model of this apartment [or house] but we're stuck with it now."

In addition to the decorators' hocus-pocus, one of the most potent appeals of these furnished models is their location. Usually they are on the edge of the first fairway or adjacent to the clubhouse or recreation center with its afore-mentioned *money magnets*. Or they may be on a small hill overlooking "the lake."

Usually, nobody tells you that the apartments or houses in "Unit Two," where you are going to buy, will be a good mile or more from all of these attractions.

Upon inquiring about distances in one of the largest of these retirement communities we were assured that there would be a free intracity bus running on frequent schedules and that "in-the-near-future" they were planning a second golf course, a second clubhouse and recreation center—and later on a third group. Not all of the things that are planned materialize. If they do, it may take some years for them to happen, depending upon how good sales are.

In any case, despite reassurances, not all of the retirees can be "just a step away" from everything—or at least not until they disprove the law that two things cannot occupy the same space at the same time—even though the inventive interior decorators seem to have managed it.

Not many people really take the trouble to ask even the minimum common-sense questions when committing themselves to such a major move. The sales forces are well trained to supply so much plausible information in such appealing form that the man who forgets to ask questions about protection against rising costs, increased taxes, insurance and medical coverage if he and his wife are away on a trip, how much of the payments are actually deductible, what the problems of resale may be in the case of emergency and so on will be tempted to shrug and say, "Oh well, everything else is so thoroughly covered that must be all right too!"

At Leisure World in Walnut Creek the sales representative anticipated this omission. Not only did he provide a thorough fill-in on the obvious points but he went on to say, "Usually there is so much to take in that folks forget to ask some very important questions. For instance, we feel that a buyer should know what his chances for resale are—in case he should find that circumstances require him to be elsewhere.

"In that connection Mr. Cortese, through his New Horizon sales organization has made arrangements to handle resales right out of this office. Even though we are building new units as fast as we can, consistent with good construction practices, we feel that there will always be a fine market for resales—*particularly if you have bought in one of the first units*.

"You see," he explained, "we do not know for certain yet, but we think that prices are going to go up by as much as $2000 for the same apartment by the time we are selling in units Two and Three. So if you were to buy now you would actually stand to show a couple of thousand dollars profit the moment you sign."

This business of hiking the prices on "Unit Two" and so on is an old gambit with tract developers and it has been carried over into retirement housing also.

Costs are discussed in the next chapter, What Price Peace? But this incident is cited now to demonstrate how much pressure, objective and subjective, is put on a person who comes wandering into this new retirement world for a look around. If you have a stray gray hair or two, and a stray dollar or two, you may find yourself trapped.

11

WHAT PRICE PEACE?

If one were to apply to retirement living the historic cartoon caption, "You pays your money and you takes your choice," it would be necessary to amend it to read, "You pays your money but there ain't much choice!"

At first glance there would seem to be. But the simple truth is not encouraging for the great mass of retired people who must live, or rather exist, on minimum incomes.

To some extent, of course, choice is implied in variety. And the impression is deliberately created that one may choose from a wide variety of such places.

Actually there are only five basic types of retirement communities:

1. The self-contained retirement city or village.
2. The urban retirement hotel or hotel-apartment.
3. The low-cost housing authority projects.
4. The mobile-home or trailer-park communities.
5. The life-care retirement facility.

They do offer a wide variety of geographic location. In a few years they will exist in some numbers in every state in the union.

It is obvious too that they must offer a wide variety of climate. *But within the financial means of any given economic group of retirees, they offer very little choice at all.* Only the very well-to-do retirees have anything resembling a wide choice of facilities. But that they always have had.

1. In the first category, the self-contained city or village, are the three Del Webb Sun City communities and Kern City. They are the pioneer retirement communities, the basic patterns upon which most of the others have developed—with some minor variations.

In this first category we also find the spectacular Ross Cortese Leisure World communities. There are presently three of them open in California, one under construction in New Jersey, another in Maryland, and one in the planning stage near Chicago. Two are in Europe, one is under way in Switzerland, and one is about to be in Italy.

Also in this category one must put Leisure Village in Lakewood, New Jersey, Friendly Valley and Leisure Town in California. There are several others of this magnitude in the preliminary planning stages and a lot more in a state of watchful waiting since there is a growing feeling—not yet fully confirmed—that the market is in danger of being overbuilt.

In terms of facilities offered it seems proper to put in the first category those large country-club-type communities that, while not strictly retirement communities or even places that make their appeals primarily to seniors, nonetheless have attracted large numbers of retirees because of their moderate prices and the extent of their recreation facilities.

Such communities are the General Development Corporation's Port St. Lucie near Stuart, Florida, and Port Charlotte on the Gulf coast of Florida.

The Mackle Brothers development at Deltona, Florida, is another such age-integrated community in which retirees may find a great variety of activity available near their modestly priced homes. On the Pacific coast the huge Rancho Bernardo development in San Diego belongs in this category.

All of these communities boast their *money magnets* and, as we have seen, these facilities are similar, if not identical, from one coast to the other. In some, the recreation and medical charges are included. In others they are optional. And in still others there are no medical plans available. In most developments buyers will have at least a half-dozen floor plans to choose from.

Some of these communities are entirely cooperative with no individual homes available. Others, perhaps the majority, offer both private homes and cooperative or condominium dwellings. This is the choice at the Del Webb Sun Cities, and the giant Tucson Green Valley development.

A few, Sacramento Manor and Walnut Creek Manor and Claremont Village, among them, offer dwellings exclusively on a rental basis with no additional charge for utilities or use of the recreation facilities.

This rental device seems to be gathering momentum. Developers in several states are now thinking in this direction rather than toward outright sale. Already there have been several spectacular failures in retirement community developments. Builders who were once thinking solely in terms of retirement communities in which homes were sold outright are proceeding with more than usual caution.

For the sake of comparison, a one-bedroom, one-bath cooperative apartment dwelling at Laguna Hills Leisure World costs $13,500. The down payment is $1187. *A forty-year, FHA-insured mortgage is mandatory.* It doesn't take much figuring to discover that a person entering Leisure World at the minimum age of fifty-two will finally achieve ownership of his cooperative share at age ninety-two! In the meantime, on the one-bedroom, one-bath apartment he will be paying from $146 to $159 a month, which includes $33.35 monthly maintenance, $5.80 monthly recreation charge which admits the resident to all of the *money magnets* including golf and horseback riding, and $34 a month for medical insurance which includes 80 per cent of those medical, surgical, hospital, and drug expenses defined in detail in the health insurance policy. In the main, it is an attractive medical plan. But since the premium is based on the number of living units, not the num-

ber of people, it is obviously a better deal for a couple than
for a widow or widower who lives alone for they, too, would
pay the full $34 monthly.

A two-bedroom, two-bath dwelling runs about $15,500 to
$17,500 with correspondingly higher monthly charges for ev-
erything except medical insurance payments.

At Del Webb's Sun City, near Riverside, in Southern
California, a one-bedroom, one-bath condominium dwelling
runs about $11,000. Maintenance runs approximately $39
monthly with all recreation facilities *except* golf included in
an additional $20 *per year* charge. For two persons who play
golf there would be an additional charge of $245 a year—$190
for one person. A major medical plan is also optional. It is
underwritten by the Continental Casualty Company and costs
about $17 per month per person for the most comprehensive
coverage offered. The cost will depend upon the options and
how much money one wishes to pay out-of-pocket (deductible) before the policy begins paying. Relatively speaking it is
a fine policy. But once again, few of these policies protect the
retiree against the really disastrous illnesses that are the cruelest teeth in The Retirement Trap. This, of course, is the per-
suasive argument used by the proponents of Medicare as an
adjunct to the present Social Security Act. The majority of the
developers seemed to feel that some form of Medicare is inevitable though none of them appeared to be in favor of it.

"We would much prefer to see this job done by private enterprise," they said, "but the economics of the problem make
it impossible for private insurance companies to shoulder the
burden alone."

Perhaps that is true. But private industry has accomplished
the impossible under pressure too many times for any thoughtful American who has faith in Yankee ingenuity to accept
that statement as *prima facie* evidence, much less as gospel
truth. Among them: industries, unions, and insurance companies certainly can do a great deal more than is presently being
done to work out methods whereby a person can *prepay* during

his productive years sufficient health insurance to take care of most of the catastrophic illnesses that deplete savings and take lives in later years. Certainly there are enough studies extant to provide the actuaries with sound data for their analyses and projections. If not, with computers there soon could be.

An officer in the Department of Health, Education and Welfare in Washington, D.C., summed up the situation by saying, "This is only a personal observation, but when I am told that the insurance companies are 'too poor' to be more generous in their allowances for these prolonged medical expenses I can only repeat what I have read in news stories in recent years, that more personal fortunes have been made in the health and accident insurance field in the past two decades than in any other enterprise. If that is true then certainly some of that profit can be ploughed back into benefits for policy-holders."

Theoretically, yes. But that would lower the stockholders' dividends and the protest would be loud and long even though they could end up paying more into Social Security to finance the government Medicare scheme.

To continue a cost comparison, at Del Webb's Sun City a two-bedroom, one-bath *private residence* can be purchased for $12,700. The down payment runs approximately $1502, including about $200 of closing costs. Interest, principal, taxes, and insurance run close to $95 a month on a conventional loan. Here again, recreation facilities cost only $20 a year per person with golf optional and extra.

A two-bedroom, *two*-bath single dwelling at the same community will cost upwards of $15,150 with $1768 down payment.

At Rancho Bernardo, the country-club community in San Diego, with a separate retirement district, a two-bedroom, one-bath single dwelling runs from $16,000 to $19,000. A two-bedroom, *two*-bath house sells from $17,000 to $22,700. There is no mandatory over-all medical insurance plan. Recreation facilities, exclusive of golf, cost $50 yearly *per residence* and a special greens fee is available to residents.

The Rancho Bernardo condominiums are competitive. The one-bedroom, one-bath apartment sells for $15,000 and the two-bedroom, *two*-bath apartment for about $20,000. On the smaller unit, the *maintenance* charges run approximately $28 monthly and on the larger units about $44.50 including taxes and insurance. This charge is added to the monthly payment of interest and principal if you do not pay cash for your unit.

Because this community is a suburb of San Diego, it enjoys certain advantages such as fine medical facilities and excellent shopping and cultural activities within a relatively short drive.

A comparison of plans taken from the best developments on both coasts indicates that there is only a negligible variation in the square feet of living space offered in comparable dwellings. The cost of land and the cost of development determines the amount of real value a builder can put into his units. In place of space, some of them offer a wider range of appliances, although in most of the furnished models the refrigerators and washer-dryers were labeled "optional."

Most of the illusion of built-in luxury is concentrated in the kitchens and bathrooms. In the latter, less than $5.00 worth of assist bars beside the toilet and in the tub and shower are sufficient to convert ordinary bathrooms into facilities "especially engineered with the older resident in mind." Another bit of this "special engineering" is the electrical outlet which has been raised from its old position on the baseboard to a position approximately thirty inches up the wall to do away with stooping. It also saves the contractor about one hundred feet of insulated wire on an average two-bedroom house.

Actually much of this "special engineering" razzle-dazzle makes sense, and when planned from the beginning it costs no more than conventional construction. But the developers spend thousands of dollars boasting about it in their newspaper ads. It is a useful gimmick. Lately nearly all tract houses for younger families have adopted some of these features. In time, shower seats and assist bars will become as commonplace as the overhead garage door and the garbage-disposal unit.

2. In the second category of retirement facility—the urban hotel or hotel-apartment exclusively devoted to the needs of the elderly—there is a somewhat wider range of choice and price.

In the older resort and urban hotels that have been converted, often by FHA-insured loans and hence under federal supervision, prices and services are surprisingly uniform. These are profit-motivated places and with good management they often give more value for the retirement dollar than the newer places—and quite often more value than some of the so-called nonprofit facilities that enjoy unusual tax advantages which one might expect to find passed along to the residents.

Two typical renovated hotels catering to the senior citizen sixty-five and over are the Blackstone Residence in Miami Beach, Florida, and the Roosevelt Hotel in Washington, D.C.

The Blackstone Residence is presided over by one of the true pioneers in the field of housing for the elderly, Michael Sossin. As executive director, Dr. Sossin (his biography says he holds an LL.D. "for his work in the new field of social gerontology") has probably accumulated more first-hand experience in the care of the elderly than any other person in the land. The 250-room Blackstone, though somewhat outdated, is filled twelve months of the year. A great many of the rooms are shared by two persons, often two widows. These are cheerful rooms in a twelve-story building just one block from the Atlantic Ocean and the best bathing area in Miami Beach.

Dr. Sossin prefers to have the Blackstone filled with retirees who have come to live on a year-round basis. But there are always a number of seasonal residents who come to spend the winter months in south Florida.

On an annual basis, one person in a room with private bath

pays $200 a month (plus Florida State Sales Tax) including three meals a day and full use of the recreation facilities.

Two persons in a room with twin beds and bath pay $125 per month each, including meals and recreation. The twelfth month is payable in advance as a surety bond.

During the season, from November to May, two persons may occupy the same room as above for $175 per month each. A single occupant must pay $250.

If a person wishes to stay for a shorter period than the usual season, there is a slight increase in charges. However, if a person wishes to spend the summer season at the Blackstone, he may do so at the lower annual rate.

When one applies for a reservation, it is possible to state any special diet requirements such as diabetic, salt-free, bland, and so forth and these special meals will be prepared under the supervision of a qualified dietician at no additional charge. A registered nurse is on duty at all times.

All in all, the Blackstone seems to meet admirably the needs of one small segment of the senior community. It is possible for one person to live there for around $2000 a year including all meals and still have money left over for a modest clothing budget and for minor medical and dental expenses.

A retired person with an income of $3500 to $4000 a year may live very well indeed in a private room with all meals paid for and still have a comfortable amount left over for medical care, clothing, and other incidentals not included in the basic charge.

If one is oriented to hotel living, the accommodations and services that the Blackstone Residence offers make a great deal of economic and psychological sense. The trouble is that there are too few operating facilities that are comparable to the Blackstone. The few account for less than one fifth of one per cent of the nation's elderly who sorely need such housing. But the number is increasing.

Prices in the more expensive places range from $500 to $1500 a month for a private suite with bath, plus meals. Also there are many other services—all extra. There was little difference between these and any conventional residential hotel in the moderate- to luxury-price ranges. In fact the only significant difference is the availability of special diets (for an extra charge) and a certain amount of supervised recreational activity. This often includes bus trips to concerts and points of interest, all of which are extra and as costly—often more so —than the conventional tourist facilities serving the same purpose. There is the advantage, worth the money to some apparently, of being with their "own group."

These expensive retirement residences serve no special need in the sociological sense. They simply prove what has been known all along—that any person with sufficient income to enjoy life's luxuries may find an infinite number of both non-profit and profit-motivated enterprises that are happy to provide them.

At the Roosevelt in Washington, D.C., Executive Director Lee Socks runs one of the newest of the renovated hotels. It is also one of the largest.

In this profit-motivated facility, owned by New York City developer Sylvan Lawrence, there was an interesting subject for study since it was the first such commercial hotel to be converted to retirement use under Section 231 of the FHA.

The Roosevelt opened its doors officially on April 16, 1963, with two registered guests. By Thanksgiving it had reached its capacity, 430. The ratio of women to men was six to four. There were only twenty-eight married couples in residence.

Retirees may come to the Roosevelt on a week-to-week basis. Said Mr. Socks, "There are two things we never ask an applicant: 'How much money do you have?' and 'How long are you going to stay?'"

Mr. Socks feels that it is wrong to place a limitation on the stay, that it is unfair to coerce older persons or to tie them down with a lease unless they demand one for their own feeling of security. "We want them to feel free," he said. "We never run a credit check on an applicant and so far we have never lost."

Lest the milk of human kindness seem abnormally sweet we might add that the Roosevelt requires one month in advance. But it is an extraordinarily good buy for a retiree with a limited income who enjoys the rather compressed society of apartment-hotel living.

The rates for double occupancy are $140 to $150 per month per person without a kitchenette. They increase to $150 to $225 per month per person with a kitchenette.

A resident desiring to occupy the room alone must pay $160 to $180 per month without a kitchenette and $185 to $230 per month with one. *All rates include two meals daily*. Each of the apartments is furnished and carpeted wall-to-wall, including the closets. Every room is centrally air-conditioned with individual controls and all bathrooms are tiled with tub-shower and the ubiquitous grab rails. There is twenty-four-hour switchboard service, weekly maid and linen service, and a number of other conveniences.

The old elevators have been replaced with new, high-speed cars, plus a service car. A special long cycle has been installed to keep the doors open in order to allow slower-moving oldsters ample time to enter and exit.

The Roosevelt is one of the very few retirement residence hotels in which the promises outlined in its brochures seem to have been kept.

As at the Blackstone in Miami Beach, the kitchen appeared to be a model example of a modern food preparation and serving center. Gleaming stainless steel and spotless tile were everywhere.

"This kitchen is operated on a franchise basis," Mr. Socks explained. "But everything is charged back, which gives me complete control of the menu. We use only the finest foods. I don't mean just good quality—I mean excellent!"

Indeed there were ample stores of nationally known brands. The meat was not frozen and was definitely top quality. All the baking was done in the Roosevelt's own bake shop with the exception of the bread. "Our dieticians arrange every kind of diet that a resident needs," said Mr. Socks. "No matter what the doctor orders for them, we will prepare it—at no extra charge."

The Roosevelt seems to be an unusually complete retirement hotel. Within its confines there is a grocery store with a surprisingly varied stock, an attractive beauty parlor, a laundry and dry cleaner, and a shoe-repair shop. Also there is a drugstore-coffee shop and an excellent cocktail lounge. A barber comes in once a week.

Two doctors maintain offices there. An office call for a resident is $3.00. There are two dentists practicing on the premises. Also a podiatrist. The fees for their services are considerably lower for residents than for others.

In the lobby there is a hobby corner where supplies may be purchased and where the handiwork of some of the more talented residents is offered for sale. As one might suspect the emphasis here is on fancy sewing, embroidery, and knitting. The shop does a brisk business and, like several of the other facilities, it is a concession operated by Mr. and Mrs. Socks.

The drugstore was well stocked but lacked many of the "five and dime" items generally found in such places.

To the question, "What are the largest selling items in here?" the clerk answered without hesitation, "Prescriptions. After that, hair tint and Serutan!"

Since the civil rights law was then being debated in Congress the question was raised concerning possible restrictions that might make it difficult for colored applicants. Mr. Socks did not answer. Instead he rose from his desk and led the way down the main hall to a large, very attractively decorated activities room. At the far end, next to the huge windows that look out on Sixteenth St. N.W., were four tables of bridge—a weekly party given by a distinguished Negro resident, Mrs. I. Letcher.

Mrs. Letcher is a retired attorney. She graduated from

Radcliffe in 1913 and embarked upon an extraordinary career that earned for her a citation from President John F. Kennedy. Long active in the League of Women Voters, Mrs. Letcher still remains close to the organization's affairs.

"The people who live here at the Roosevelt simply do not understand all this fuss about integration," said Mr. Socks. "We have been integrated completely and happily ever since the day we opened. It required no federal regulation. It is the way we want it. It works so beautifully that we simply do not think about it around here—unless someone asks."

It was obvious that, here at least, the question had been satisfactorily answered by demonstration. At that time, the Roosevelt had about a dozen Negro residents.

As for religion, the residents were divided about equally— one third Catholic, one third Protestant, and one third Jewish.

Of course the most dependable way to find the truth about any retirement facility is to engage in a series of informal conversations with residents, preferably those with whom one strikes up a casual acquaintance.

While waiting for Mr. Socks to finish an interview, a rare opportunity occurred to appraise the Roosevelt.

An old gentleman was sitting in the lobby doing a little "people watching"—a favorite pastime in most of these hotels. (Mr. Socks limits the number of chairs to discourage cluttering the lobby with sitters who sometimes doze off and snore!)

A second older gentleman approached him. Both men belonged to a passing generation of Middle European immigrants in whom courtesy is deeply ingrained. The following is an exact transcript of their brief encounter.

Newcomer: (Approaching somewhat timidly) Good morning.
Resident: (Looking up) Good morning.
Newcomer: You don't mind if I ask? You live here?
Resident: (Nodding) I live here.
Newcomer: Could I ask how long?
Resident: I'm here five months.

Newcomer: Do you like it?

Resident: Are you looking?

Newcomer: Yes. Anyway, I've got the money to pay.

Resident: I like it. It's very good. Very good.

Newcomer: How is the food?

Resident: Very good.

Newcomer: Do you have special food . . . ?

Resident: Special . . . ? What is "special"?

Newcomer: "Special" is low sodium—low fat.

Resident: I eat anything.

Newcomer: Lucky! *I* got a diet.

Resident: (Nodding understandingly) They'll fix it for you. It's very nice here, believe me.

Newcomer: (Looking around) Lots of old ladies, eh?

Resident: More than old men.

Newcomer: That makes it friendly . . . ?

Resident: (With feeling) That makes it friendly!

Newcomer: Well—I thank you for your time.

Resident: Don't mention. It's all I got.

Newcomer: Likewise—well—good day.

Resident: It's the truth I'm telling you. It's very nice here. Good day.

Not all of the hotel-apartment-type retirement accommodations are well run. Unhappily there are many—some not very much less expensive than the good examples cited—that pretend to offer approximately the same services and recreation facilities but do it shamefully if indeed they do it at all.

They are not hard to find in most of the large cities. Many of them are old multiple dwellings or hotels in poor districts and are depressing in the extreme. They ranged from second best to shabby. The worst of them are "warehouses for the living dead" as one welfare worker described them. Certainly they are warehouses of hopelessness and "dumping grounds" for the unwanted old folks. In them, one may see tragic loneliness, rejection, and futility. Truly these elders are "the abandoned."

In the worst of these places management greeted inquiries with suspicion or outright hostility. Most questions remained unanswered and thus, tacitly, were answered with revealing clarity.

"Look," said one gouging operator of a shameful place on the fringe of New York City, "I run this dump for money! It is a dirty business, keeping these old people. They are pigs. I earn every buck I can get. If the wife and I didn't run this place out of the goodness of our hearts these old b————s would be in the County Work House!"

To which one might add that if these old ones could qualify, they'd be infinitely better off in any senior facility operated by the city or state of New York. New York City's housing authority program is among the best in the world. Happily, new state laws and local ordinances are beginning to clean up some of the worst of these private retirement facilities run by predatory landlords. But so long as greed and avarice remain fundamental elements in human nature there will be among us those who set principle aside for profit. Where conscience and responsibility are present few restraining laws are needed. Where they are not present some central authority must provide the intended victims with protection against the unprincipled operators. As the elderly market increases in size the combined purchasing power of the widow's mite will become mighty indeed. And so will the temptation to exploit it.

There is a growing trend on the part of some developers to make use of FHA's Section 231 in order to secure government insurance on the huge loans needed to refurbish and often redesign these older hotels and apartments for retirement living. If the trend develops, it seems likely that a more realistic set of minimum standards will evolve in the federally insured places. Certain basic standards are at present a prime condition for securing FHA loan insurance. But despite care in setting these minimum requirements under Section 231, the FHA seems somewhat unrealistic at times.

For instance, in many of the larger retirement hotel-apartments equipped with efficiency kitchens, gas stoves were required or at least condoned. Managing directors all agreed that this is dangerous. Older persons are apt to become forgetful or victims of failing hearing and eyesight. An accidentally opened gas jet, an unseen or unheard boil-over, or a flame blown out by a draught not only can but already has taken the lives of many elders in private dwellings. Indeed, escaping gas is a common cause of household accidents, involving even much younger homemakers.

Most retirement-facility operators felt that electric stoves and heating should be mandatory. Of course, under certain circumstances, electricity can be dangerous too. But in the cooking and heating applications it was agreed that it offers fewer hazards to the elderly than toxic and explosive household gas.

3. The third category, the low-cost housing authority projects designed especially for, or arranged to incorporate the elderly, offers one of the really promising solutions to the greatest part of the retirement housing problem.

Most large American cities and some small ones have taken effective steps toward providing modern dwellings for those sixty-five years of age and over who must live on minimum incomes derived principally from Social Security, modest pensions, or small family remittances.

The majority of the public housing projects are city-initiated, though some receive impetus from state funds and some are federally aided. The requirements for entrance are remarkably uniform.

New York City is the leader in the number of such housing authority projects. There were eighty-four projects operating or scheduled to be in operation by the beginning of 1965. They are scattered throughout the five boroughs and they range from pioneer projects in Manhattan and Brooklyn to the newest concepts in public housing rising in the Bronx.

One building in the Van Dyke complex in Brooklyn and one in the Gaylord White complex in Manhattan are designed especially for the elderly and represent one of the great steps forward in meeting their needs. Elderly persons are also integrated in other low-cost housing authority projects. In some instances special floors have been set aside for them in general family dwellings.

Entrance requirements are uniform but income limits vary from project to project. According to a bulletin released by the N.Y.C. Housing Authority the general, maximum income limits for admission of elderly single persons may be as high as $3600 a year in federally aided developments, and as high as $4104 for admission to state-aided developments.

For a two-person family, income may be as high as $4720 per year for admission to federally aided developments, and as high as $5544 for admission to state-aided developments. Certain deductions are allowed in figuring family income. These include pension costs, Social Security payments, and union dues.

In New York City, these limits may be increased up to $800 for a secondary wage earner. In state-aided developments income limits for persons who receive pension or Social Security payments may be increased up to $900 for a one-person family and up to $1800 for a two-person family.

For families composed of two or more members there are no age requirements for admission to public housing. In the case of a one-person family (single-person occupancy) a person must be at least fifty years of age for admission to a state-aided development. For admission to a federally aided development a person must be at least sixty-two years of age unless he is disabled pursuant to the definition of the Social Security Act.

In Cleveland, Ohio, world-renowned for its progressive solutions to the low-rent housing needs of its citizens, there are

7400 dwellings on fourteen sites. These are completed and occupied, according to Ernest J. Bohn, director of the Cleveland Metropolitan Housing Authority and an acknowledged pioneer and major figure in the field. In addition there are a hundred more dwellings under construction on still another site with more in the planning stage.

Families who, without financial assistance, are unable to obtain decent homes at rents they can afford to pay and who are now living in substandard housing or who are being evicted through no fault of their own are eligible for admission, as are single persons sixty-two years of age and over.

The annual net family income cannot exceed $3000 per year plus $200 for each minor dependent. When the income exceeds this amount by $660, the resident is asked to vacate and is given six months to do so.

Regardless of the size of the dwelling or size of the family, the rent is approximately 23 per cent of the *net* family income. In most cases the rent includes some or all of the utilities.

In all of the housing developments or "estates" built by the Cleveland Metropolitan Housing Authority, recreational centers and health facilities have been provided. There is also a well-staffed elderly clinic where preventive medical examinations may be had.

One feature of the Cleveland approach to housing for the elderly is the Golden Age Center, in which a number of different recreational opportunities are provided for a very small monthly sum.

As in New York City, the Cleveland Metropolitan Housing Authority, under Chairman H. Stuart Harrison, has taken pains not to isolate the elderly. In most of its facilities there are special accommodations designed with the needs of the elderly resident in mind but these older citizens need never feel isolated or "tucked away" from the younger members of society. In their own quarters, however, they may be *insulated* from the full force of youthful enthusiasm, as in the tower apartments adjacent to the garden apartments provided for families with children.

As of 1964, Cleveland's total investment in its remarkable housing program totals only slightly over $62.5 million, or less than 10 per cent of just one single widely publicized government aid program to a foreign country that has announced its intention of stabbing us in the back at the first opportunity. One could wish that the needy—particularly the needy elderly citizens of our own country—could be given the same priority.

In the newest public housing projects, advances in design are making it easier for authorities to overcome a long-time resistance on the part of some of the elderly to move into what they often term "institutionalized" dwellings.

Cleveland's "estates" have attracted world-wide attention for their effectiveness in breaking down this prejudice. That it still exists is evident in a letter received by the National Council on the Aging in New York City. Beverly Diamond, consultant on Housing and Community Planning, feels the following letter typifies the attitude of many older persons who have been long accustomed to their own apartments or private residences. The letter reads in part:

I want to tell you what it is like to be old. I am a 72 year old widow, a former buyer for a department store, and have lived in the same four-room apartment for 35 years. It is a pleasant, light apartment. I like this old building [in N.Y.C.]. The halls are clean, there is always enough heat.

Up to now I have had an income of $2,900.00 a year. In the last several years I have earned a little extra by writing fashion news for the trade. Since my husband's death, however, I have found it difficult to pay the $97.00 per month rent.

My son, who is married and has two children in college, visits me, especially on holidays. Sometimes he gives me money to help pay the doctor bills.

For the last year, however, going down to purchase the

newspaper or the necessary journals has been an ordeal. You see, I have developed arthritis and have to climb three flights of stairs, plus the steep stone steps of the stoop outside. What was charming before is now a trap.

It is even worse when I have to get groceries. The grocery store that used to deliver an order is gone.

I asked the landlord for a lower apartment which became vacant, but he said he would be entitled to more rent if I moved downstairs, even though the apartment would be smaller and the building is rent controlled. I even thought of sacrificing the phone and trying it, but then I could not get calls from my grandchildren and the few friends I seldom see.

Once in a while I manage to go to my church, but frankly I am ashamed since I do not even have the money to chip in like others for the many good works we do.

I always loved this town—its many opportunities to touch life in many ways, to pursue, to do and sometimes even to rue, the vitality of its streets, the excitement of ever-present change. Now, when I walk cautiously down the block, a break in the pavement, a tricycle, a shopping cart, a slight slope, two people walking abreast, a high curb, the swiftly changing traffic light, all are a menace. I used to look up and see friendly faces and stop to chat. Now I see only the rears of air conditioners. The neighborliness has been drained from the neighborhood. Parking lots have taken the place of brownstones and cars dart out without warning.

Everytime I go out, I sit at the bottom landing and cry and every day I feel a little less a person. I would like to get the kind of apartment I have read about. *I do not mean the large public projects which frighten me.*[1] I mean some place where I can be with others my own age, carry on a conversation, make new friends, do things together, maybe even see a show again. I would be able to pay $80.00 a month to do this. Can you help me?

[1] Authors' italics.

The Commissioner's Standard Ordinary Tables for 1958 used by most of the large insurance companies in this country to project life expectancies show that on the average a woman seventy-two years of age will live approximately 9.15 more years.

The law of probabilities indicates that this widow who has written such an eloquent plea to the National Council on the Aging will endure an increasingly agonized existence for at least that much longer.

When it is remembered that nearly 90 per cent of the 18.7 million seniors in the country are seventy years or older and that an overwhelming majority of them are in the lowest income brackets, the urgency of this woman's plea may be understood.

In commenting on this particular case, Beverly Diamond had this to say in part:

Unfortunately . . . public housing can never meet the total need of even the lowest income group. With several hundred thousand dwelling units already built, there are still problems.

Our correspondent, it is true, meets the income requirements of low-income housing—if you could convince her to accept the public project.

But—public housing must set priorities. The first right for such housing is usually given to the large number of elderly persons dislocated by slum clearance and urban renewal or who have no housing whatsoever. Second priority is given to those who live in what is termed "unsatisfactory housing." This is usually taken to mean substandard housing, detrimental to the health of the individual or family.

Only a very few persons with serious heart conditions, living in standard housing, are admitted to public housing, and then only with considerable substantiation from hospital or doctor and with the social worker's persistence. These priorities are valid in view of the large number of applications that usually flood public housing. *The chances of our correspondent are slim indeed!*

This vast army of aging, ailing veterans of the struggle for survival is increasing at the rate of a quarter of a million persons a year. Even if only half were eligible, the increase in any one year would be over ten times the ability of public housing to provide for them when projected on the present rate of building. On the face of it the problem would seem to be a hopeless one. And still it is within the realm of possibility to solve a great part of it without resorting to the methods of the welfare state. A suggestion as to how this might be accomplished in succeeding generations will be discussed in the last chapter.

New York City's Public Housing projects have been used as a representative model for examination here. But splendid public housing facilities exist in most large cities and in an increasing number of smaller ones such as Reno, Nevada, already noted. Victoria Plaza in San Antonio, Texas, is also an outstanding example of modern, low-cost public housing.

It would be folly to attempt to list the hundreds of others in these pages. Their omission implies neither tacit criticism nor lack of interest. It means, quite simply, that space does not permit a full examination of them all since they vary only slightly from one city to another.

Before these pages reach the press, a directory will be available through The National Council on the Aging, 49 West 45 St., New York City. It will contain the most complete and detailed listing of senior citizen residential facilities in the nation. The purpose of this book is not to duplicate that service but rather to evaluate the principal types of living facilities presently available to senior citizens and to do so by citing as examples those projects which we believe to be typical of each category.

4. The fourth type of retirement community concept is the mobile home or trailer park that purports to make available "gracious living" at extremely low cost. Some of them do. Oth-

ers have become so elaborate that it is a matter of preference, not dollars, as to whether one lives in a commodious trailer complete with two bedrooms, two baths, and all of the *money magnets* available, including swimming pools and championship golf courses, or whether one simply buys a conventional home or apartment in a Leisure World- or Sun City-type community.

Dozens of these trailer parks were visited. Most of them were inhabited by mobile-minded seniors who simply preferred that mode of living to houses. Many of them seemed to resent the tendency to lump their little "tin-box towns," as one columnist terms them, with the out-and-out retirement communities.

"We ain't been put out to pasture here," said salty old Bill Barkham in St. Petersburg, Florida. "We come here because we wanted to. Lots of us work a little. But mostly we just fish and take it easy. We earned it. We planned it this way. And if we feel like it we can always pull up stakes and trail our home to Phoenix, Arizona, or to Long Beach, California, or anywhere else we take a fancy to. We're independent!" he said emphatically, "and we sure as hell don't want to be lumped up with them old people!"

When asked his age, Bill replied proudly, "I'm seventy-three. But there's seventy-three and seventy-three. Inside I'm mostly about fifty-three." And then with a parchment crinkling around his fisherman's blue eyes, he added, "On a good day that is!"

But beneath the bright, restless surface of conviviality and independence, there seems to be a dark shadow of uncertainty and insecurity among many of these mobilites. They work hard at reassuring themselves. They do this by fostering the belief that any time they want to they can "pull up stakes" and trail to a greener pasture.

Actually, in the more elaborate residential trailer parks very few of them do. These so-called mobile homes, surrounded as they are by built-ons such as added rooms, front, side, and rear porches, and ramadas, to say nothing of landscaping and adjacent storage huts, would require as much effort and expense to "pull up stakes" and trail as it would to move a six-room house. Comforting as the thought may be, most of this prized mobility is a myth.

Many of these mobilized seniors do keep a small camping trailer out back. When the urge to hit the open road becomes uncontrollable, they can close up the large trailer homes, hitch up, and take off across the country.

There are thousands of trailer clubs, mostly formed and enjoyed by persons in their middle to late years. These clubs combat boredom and satisfy the urge to wander by planning trips and get-togethers. Several times while researching our recent Doubleday book, *The Simple Truth about Western Land Investment,* we came across such conclaves.

Some of the most ubiquitous groups are those owners of Wally Byam Airstream Trailers who seem to take a special pride in their gleaming, loaf-shaped aluminum vehicles. One such was discovered at road's end in the Mount Baker Primitive Area in North Central Washington State. This particular group seemed somewhat younger but it contained more than a sprinkling of elders.

"A time will come," said one of these seniors, "when we can't make these trips into unspoiled country. So we're hot-footing it around with the younger ones as much as we can now. Except for gas and oil, it doesn't cost any more than staying at home."

For those senior citizens who are physically and temperamentally attuned to a roving retirement, there is a great deal of geographical variety in such a life. Certainly a retired couple of means, traveling by train or airline and depending upon established hotel and resort facilities for food and shelter, would spend many more dollars to enjoy fewer tourist attractions. Moreover, it is doubtful if the well-heeled ones who take conveniences for granted would find as much pleasure in the coming and going.

Of course a great many of these merry mobilites come from

conventional homes and simply use the smaller, truly mobile trailers as a compact but comfortable means of keeping living costs down during their vacation trips. A drive through any of the Del Webb retirement cities will reveal a large number of such open-road trailers. The same is true of both Port St. Lucie and Port Charlotte, Florida.

But it remained for the loquacious Art Linkletter, master showman and financier, to develop the last word in luxurious mobile-home retirement within reach of the modestly moneyed senior citizen.

Linkletter calls his retirement village Sierra Dawn. It is located within the city limits of Hemet, California, about midway between San Diego and Los Angeles. Hence it enjoys all of the conveniences of urban living. For many years the area has been known as one of the most beautiful in Southern California. While it may fall a bit short of the mythical Shangri-La, it is, nonetheless, a sort of scaled-down Vale of Kashmir with its lush green fields and its backdrop of 10,000-foot snow-capped peaks. There is reasonable evidence that the area enjoys some of the most salubrious climate in the hemisphere. The town of Hemet itself is rich in Indian lore. In fact, the annual Ramona Pageant, during which is enacted the tragedy of Ramona and Allesandro, attracts thousands of visitors to the presentation's striking, natural amphitheater.

Next to agriculture, the Hemet Valley's second great economic asset is its retirees. The first of them began seeking its mild climate and natural hot springs before the turn of the century.

Linkletter's Sierra Dawn is not alone in the area. Several other mobile retirement communities are building or are planned. But the famous showman's is the largest and at the moment the most elaborate. Minimum age for residence is fifty.

This sort of development must not be confused with the ordinary trailer park with its rather skimpy rental "pads" and the untidy bouquets of umbilical connections to sewers and utilities.

At Sierra Dawn the average lot is 48 by 85 feet. None is smaller than 45 by 80 feet and the largest will run about 62 by 100 feet. This latter dimension compares favorably with the R-1 lots in many a well-planned conventional town or suburb.

In order to keep Sierra Dawn from becoming a motley collection of "galloping lunch boxes," as one builder called them, the management has placed a minimum size limit on the mobile homes that may be accepted. Each home must be at least 40 by 10 feet (400 square feet), although some exceptions may be made by management after inspection of the unit.

Owners may improve the lots with landscaping as they desire, but Sierra Dawn reserves the right to approve certain large plantings and fencing despite the fact that the buyer purchases the lot outright. Anyone keeping cats and dogs need not apply. Presumably parakeets, canaries, and well-spoken myna birds would be welcome.

Unlike many mobile-home communities Sierra Dawn boasts dedicated city streets. The trailers are numbered as conventional city residences and mail is delivered to each owner's lot. In short, much is offered here that is not usually found in mobile communities.

Here again is demonstrated the remarkable efficacy of the *money magnets*. They cost money—and in the end it is the customer's money. The practice is rather like asking the fish to cut his own bait. Considering the attractiveness of the lures, it is not surprising that a lot of these fish are happy to pay for the privilege of being hooked. We certainly do not imply that any of those hooked are suckers . . . most especially not at Sierra Dawn.

Art Linkletter's *money magnets* run true to form. They are numerous and of extremely high quality. And several times a year Art throws himself into the bargain when he becomes the master of ceremonies of Sierra Dawn's shows that celebrate some major holiday or other special occasion. As one dreamy-eyed lady said, "My idea of heaven would be to have Mr. Link-

letter host the show with Lawrence Welk as the guest star!"
Since Welk is no mean financier himself it comes as no sur-
prise then to find that he has a retirement community of his
own in Escondido, California. These men from show business
have a potent built-in appeal for thousands of customers. And
let it not be forgotten that the basic social ingredient in all
of these retirement communities is the predilection for the
"homey" pleasures that show business has long since recognized as powerful appeals and labeled "corn." Properly culti-
vated there is nothing bantam about it and most certainly it
can be golden!

Lots at Sierra Dawn average about $5000. On these one
may put a mobile home costing on the average from about
$6500 for a one-bedroom, one-bath unit to $13,000 for a
two-bedroom, two-bath unit.

This means the price range for a complete mobile home
with lot but exclusive of planting, fencing, and screened in
lanai can run from $11,500 to $18,000 and more, plus furnishings. Ramadas, parking shelters, and outdoor storage cabi-
nets can add several hundred dollars to the price.

These prices, then, come very close to those for the same
basic living space found in conventional retirement housing.
But at Sierra Dawn at least there appears to be some advantage in monthly maintenance and recreational charges.

In one of the fact sheets provided by the sales representative, management points out, "the immediate advantage of
owning your own lot (at Sierra Dawn) is that you do not pay
the park owner a profit in the form of rent." The sheet suggests
that costs to the owner of a *free and clear* lot total less than
$25 per month. The breakdown is given as follows:

Water	$3.00
Trash and garbage	1.25
Taxes	3.00
Recreation center	15.00
Total	$22.25 monthly

However, a lot and mobile home purchased on time payments can add considerably to that minimum outlay. In one instance the financing on the lot came to $66 monthly after the normal down payment of 25 per cent. The monthly charges on a two-bedroom, two-bath trailer came to $188, making a total of $276.25. In addition, most states charge a substantial, annual, vehicle license fee plus a registration fee. The license fee is usually based on 2 per cent of the retail value of the mobile home. There is a depreciation allowance.

An impressive number of Sierra Dawn residents, it was said, owned expensive homes prior to buying there. In many cases they had been able to sell them for a nice profit, which often resulted in a Sierra Dawn home free and clear with a nice nest egg to boot. In such cases the $22.25 a month for water, trash, land taxes, and recreation adds up to a modest overhead sum even when one adds about $20 per year per thousand dollars of value for the vehicle tax. On a $10,000 trailer home this would add another $16 or so a month to the budget, bringing the total charge to approximately $38.25 a month . . . still a very modest amount.

In most of the retirement communities around the country, management always could point with pride to at least one resident who was "making out nicely" on Social Security alone. Sierra Dawn was no exception. It also boasted the most elaborately decorated mobile home in the world, a promotional gambit in which the interior decorator really outdid himself. This spectacular example of decorating hocus-pocus deservedly wound up in a feature color-photo layout in the Los Angeles *Times Home* magazine and reportedly attracted a lot of lookers and supposedly some buyers. The bemused sales representative agreed that it was about as "far out" as an interior decorator could get—at least in a trailer.

But again—mobile-home living, as it is capriciously called, is a misnomer. As we pointed out, the most elaborate of these trailers is about as mobile as the Empire State Building.

The largest of them (approximately 20 by 60 feet), although technically wheel-bearing vehicles, never touch the road at all. Very often they are shipped in two halves aboard special "wide-load" rigs. At the destination they are set directly on permanent foundations and bolted together. In California, for instance, just so long as the wheels remain attached to the chassis these mobile homes may enjoy a really substantial property tax advantage. Consequently when the foundation is made, a hole is dug for the wheels so the body of the not-so-mobile home may rest on the new support without losing its technical tax advantage.

Although powerful lobbies are fighting it, there is a move afoot in some areas to tax these huge mobile homes on much the same basis as any conventional home set up on a regular building site. The first breakthrough came in January of 1965, when the Florida State Supreme Court declared unconstitutional the state law exempting residential trailers from a personal property tax. In searching for new sources of revenue it is expected other states will soon follow suit, thereby depriving residential trailers of one of their prime advantages.

At Sierra Dawn there is a flat recreation charge of $15 a month, excluding golf, which at the moment may be played on a very attractive neighborhood course in Hemet.

Linkletter's group says it has invested more than $300,000 in Sierra Dawn's recreation center and anyone who sees it will not doubt that statement. It is equipped with all of the standard *money magnets* and then some. The $15 monthly charge is all-inclusive. There are no other charges for using any of the facilities, including the very complete hobby shops. But there is one important difference: Sierra Dawn owns the recreation center, maintains it, and administers it. Management promises that it will assume this responsibility in perpetuity.

In most of the large retirement communities these recreation facilities (with golf courses excepted in some cases) are eventually turned over to an association of home owners who then must assume the entire responsibility of operating and administering their elaborate facilities. Under good committee management—a rare thing—costs to members may remain substantially as they were at the outset. But with everything becoming more expensive it also seems likely that these recreation charges can and probably will increase within the foreseeable future. At Sierra Dawn it was stated that this could not happen. A little rough arithmetic would seem to confirm this: the 371 lots in the map of the first unit could produce, when sold, about $66,780 per year gross income based on the $15 monthly recreation charge per lot.

It was stated that the entire recreation facility was operated by three employees. Even allowing for utilities, maintenance, and payroll it would appear that this facility can more than earn its own way. It would also appear to be a wise management decision to keep it, despite the possibility of a cost-of-living increase.

So, as alluring as the *money magnets* are, nothing is really "given away" in these retirement communities. The residents pay for everything, one way or another. But the methods of extracting these profits have been so refined that by comparison painless dentistry is as crude as the rack.

We come now to the fifth category. We had planned to give it a paragraph. But upon investigation, it was decided to devote a special chapter to it—in fact, two of them!

12

LET US PREY?

"God bless you, folks! God bless you for bringing your wonderful old mother in to see us. We feel that when good Christians such as you wander in off the street to make inquiry about our retirement home you don't really 'wander in' at all—you are led!

"Everything happens according to His great blueprint. That is how this blessed retirement home came to pass too. We were led to found it. And we feel that every dear old soul who has entrusted us with her worldly goods so that she may live here in peace and contentment in the golden evening of her life was also led here by God's own hand!"

The foregoing oozed from the unctuous executive director of one of the scores of tax-favored, nonprofit, church-oriented and fraternal institutions that are springing up in every state in the Union. The Christian churches—particularly the Protestant denominations—appear to have a virtual monopoly on these so-called nonprofit life-care homes for the retired.

Some of them are really excellent and in them may be found inspiring examples of charity and dedication to the welfare of the needy elderly in the lower-income brackets. But many of them resemble out-and-out businesses that exploit their special economic advantages to compete for the rich new retirement market. Their account books show no profit as such. But nonetheless they are able to find the credit to acquire vast new holdings of prime property and to build upon it some of the most modern and luxurious retirement homes in the world, catering almost entirely to that small segment of our senior citizenry called the affluent elderly.

If the advantages of easier and cheaper mortgage insurance, and small or virtually no taxes were actually being passed along in all cases in the form of lower rates and increased services that would help the needy elders who comprise the majority of our senior citizenry, it would be a very pleasant task, indeed a duty, to sing their praises to high heaven. But the sad truth is—many of them are not.

Certainly this does not include such organizations as the Soroptimists, who operate nonprofit, low-cost senior housing comparable in every way to the finest public housing projects in the nation.

Modest starts in Florida and in California are proving successful and the feminine service club envisions many such homes for the aged across the land.

There are no entrance fees. Qualifications are much the same as those for public housing projects. While no medical plan is offered, the Soroptimists have located their pioneer projects very near fine medical facilities.

Rentals run approximately $45 for a single studio apartment and $55 for a one-bedroom apartment. This leaves the average senior on Social Security some funds for other basic necessities.

Occupants must carry medical insurance or they must be eligible for Old Age Assistance. They need not belong to any special ethnic, religious, or club groups. All in all it would seem that this particular endeavor is conforming to both the spirit of the enabling laws and the most commendable definition of a private organization's responsibility to the community.

With the exception of a few truly public-spirited groups, most of these nonprofit retirement homes seem to be in direct competition with the highly taxed private developers for the growing market of seniors in the upper-middle and upper-income brackets—the brackets that comprise what the Research Institute of America labels "the golden age" communities of "the opulent elderly."

The finest of the new nonprofit, church- and foundation-sponsored homes are going up in the largest cities, usually on the most expensive land in the choicest locations, to provide what amounts to luxurious carefree living for thousands of elderly persons who are in want of nothing but congenial company of their own age and income levels. When one is exposed to a number of these retired elderly in this new environment it is impossible to escape the impression that in the most luxurious of these places there is prevalent a particularly insidious form of clublike snobbery.

A group of nonprofit, tax-favored, church-associated retirement facilities was contrasted with a comparable group of profit-motivated ventures. The facilities and real estate values of both groups were approximately the same. And so were the prices charged by each for similar services, despite the fact that the profit-motivated enterprises enjoyed no tax-forgiveness advantages and also were forced to pay more for their investment money and for their mortgage insurance. Moreover, in addition to comparable monthly fees, the nonprofit retirement facilities required rigorous physical examinations to guarantee that the applicants are ambulatory and not likely to require expensive protracted nursing for which the home would be obligated. Also they demanded cash "founder's fees" ranging from $7000 to $50,000!

While the profit-motivated group pays its fair share of taxes into the economy for the privilege of doing business and competing for this huge new market, the nonprofit places contribute little or nothing in taxes and often are able to secure up to 100 per cent financing and 100 per cent FHA insurance on their loans. In a number of instances these retirement homes used loans to acquire additional valuable land which, once purchased, was effectively removed from the public tax rolls. Once this is accomplished the land contributes virtually nothing to the support of the community that makes the very existence of these places possible. In far too many instances these places contribute neither an equitable share of taxes nor adequate services to the lower-income group of elderly who often must depend wholly or in part upon community assistance financed directly or indirectly by the taxpayer.

To be sure, the nonprofit places often keep a nonpaying guest or two on the books. Some of these so-called charity cases are actually persons who had paid thousands for their life-care contracts and then had fooled the actuaries by outliving the projections. It does happen—but not often.

One old fellow—past ninety—has taken particular delight in needling the management of one such place in Southern California. Each morning he makes it a point to pass the manager's office. If the door is open he peers in, clicks his false teeth happily, and says, "Well, Reverend—this is another day on the house!"

There is no accurate count of the total of such nonprofit, church-oriented or church-inspired or church-motivated or church-associated or church-affiliated places. There are several directories, but as of the beginning of 1965 these were not up to date, so quickly are the various denominations moving to secure a share of this expanding market.

In more pious parlance it is not called a market but rather "an opportunity to serve." In most instances the homes take great pains to make it known that they are affiliated with such-and-such a church or denomination. But in many instances under careful questioning they take equal pains to make it clear that the denomination does not *operate* the incorporated facility but merely "expedited" its founding by placing its "blessings" on same and in some cases by advancing modest sums to get it started.

But whatever the relationship, a review of the directories available indicates a possible total of some fifteen hundred such nonprofit retirement homes in the United States. Even if the very modest sum of a half million dollars is assigned to each the result would be a total investment of three quarters of a billion dollars—largely tax free. The actual figure is said to be many times that. The administrator of one West Coast chain operation admitted that their half dozen or so homes alone represented an investment of $40 million. He and his church-oriented organization are obviously proud of their sheer size and material wealth, in much the same manner, it seemed, that a great industry might be proud of its size and material wealth.

In Washington, D.C., no unequivocal answer was forthcoming from the FHA as to why these church-, foundation-, and fraternally motivated, nonprofit retirement facilities should enjoy financial advantages. One official spoke vaguely of their "exalted mission and high dependability factor" and another spoke with equal vagueness of "the very great service they render to the needy."

But spokesmen for the National Council on the Aging in New York City and the Department of Health, Education and Welfare in Washington were more specific:

"For the most part," they said, "these places are taking care of people who don't need assistance. The ones who really need help are being left to shift for themselves!"

Dr. Donald Kent, Director of the Office of Aging of H.E.W., made this observation:

"Among those who are able to help the elderly, in a youth-centered society, too much emphasis is being placed on having fun in our golden years—the country-club concept of retirement that cannot possibly help the millions of less fortunate elders who must exist on the lowest incomes."

Without exception, however, even in the most elaborate of these nonprofit, church-motivated retirement homes, the managers and administrators took pains to point out their perpetually precarious financial positions. Not once but many times this statement was made:

"Nonprofit retirement facilities are in dire danger of going under because we are giving so much more than we are able to get due to fixed life-care fees, leases, and other agreements that were unrealistic in the light of our present cost of living increases."

If this is true, then how does it happen that the similar *profit-motivated retirement facilities—without the advantage of a founder's fee—*are still thriving (with waiting lists in many) on fees that are not only comparable to the nonprofit charges but often are lower for similar services in the same general environment?

If this is true, then how does it happen that the largest increase in applications for FHA loan insurance both for renovation and for new construction is to be found in the tax-exempt, nonprofit retirement facilities?

Are these groups really all standing in line to perpetuate a bad bargain? Or are they afraid that some day soon the American taxpayer is going to grow weary of his increasing burden and begin looking at those who have been enjoying a privileged, tax-sheltered position in our economy and hence wish to acquire as much property as possible before the advent of that lesser "Judgment Day"?

During an interview with the reverend administrator of one of the most luxurious new church-associated nonprofit manors in northern California we were told that anticipated reserves from his highly successful new venture would be used to build additional facilities adjacent to the present ones.

When we asked what would happen if the forces that oppose nonprofit corporation tax forgiveness were to prevail, this personable and able business administrator replied, "It would eliminate the segment who need help most and would throw these old people on state care."

At this particular manor a number of delightful elderly couples were interviewed. They had paid upwards of $15,000 for lifetime use of a beautiful two-room apartment. In addition they pay $190 monthly subsistence fee *per person.* Obviously these couples have retirement incomes well above the median-income levels for their groups. In their present circumstances they hardly seem to be persons who are likely to end up as public charges.

Another administrator said, "The politicians who are trying to gain attention in the press by making sponsored corporations pay property taxes are going to have a fight on their hands!"

"Why?" we asked.

"Because if we have to pay full property taxes it would amount to a couple of hundred dollars a year per resident above what we are getting from them now. In our various retirement homes we have almost two thousand residents. That means another four or five hundred thousand dollars a year. Once a contract is signed here, we can't up it."

When asked if paying full property taxes would create a financial crisis the answer was, "No—not an actual crisis—but we would not be able to operate at our present level. We'd have to cut down on some of our services until the old contracts run out. Then we'd have to up the ante on new contracts to make up the difference."

"How," we asked, "does a contract run out?"

"A contract runs out when a resident leaves us—or dies . . . mostly the latter."

We asked if any of the church-related corporations would oppose legislation to force them to pay property taxes.

"Certainly," the administrator replied, "we would do everything possible to call this unfair political assault on charity work to the attention of our residents and their families. I should think," he added, "that our residents could muster quite a bit of dedicated Christian opposition at the polls. I should think it would be in the nature of a crusade!"

True, an eventual loss of tax advantage could mean that a few showcase charity residents might be thrown on relief and costs would generally rise. But if a nonprofit place has been set up on as sound a business basis as a successfully run and comparable profit-motivated place, then why would any radical change be forced on those residents who are paying their way?

There is no intent here to imply that there is anything legally wrong with providing comfortable, even luxurious, surroundings for retired persons who can afford to pay. There is a definite intent, however, to give the lie to the often deliberately encouraged impression that most of these tax-exempt or tax-favored nonprofit retirement homes are performing a much-needed service, often in the name of charity, and therefore are deserving of special consideration in taxation and financing.

There seems little, if any, reluctance on the part of the governing boards to fix charges for services that are well in line with those being charged for comparable services by profit-motivated facilities, some of which operate efficiently on a 2 per cent net return—*after taxes*.

At another church-motivated retirement life-care residence near San Diego, California, we spoke with still another clergy-man who had forsaken the pulpit for the administrator's desk.

Here again, in the midst of truly breath-taking surroundings being enjoyed by senior residents of more than average means (with the exception of the several ubiquitous "charity" cases), the harrowing tale of brinkmanship financing was heard again. And again management pointed with pride to its newest acquisitions. These proved to be some of the area's most expensive urban real estate on which was being constructed additional ultramodern housing for the affluent elderly.

One couple, well in their seventies, were patiently waiting for construction to be completed on a new cottage that the home was building—a cottage they had reserved for the rest of their lives for a fee of $38,000 in addition to the usual monthly charges, which were estimated to be in excess of $500. Certainly nobody would begrudge this delightful couple the luxury they are able to afford. But clearly these two persons are not in any immediate danger of becoming charity cases either.

Dr. Kent, in his discussion of the problems of the aging, indicated a condition in our society that one might expect would inspire some truly "Christian charity" on the part of those whose various advantages might make them better able to serve.

"Thirty per cent of the poverty groups in the United States are elderly. And thirty per cent of the wealthy groups in the country are also elderly," he observed.

Assuming these figures to be reasonably correct, is it then *unreasonable* to suggest that a *fully taxed profit-motivated* enterprise might continue to make its contribution to our socio-economic welfare by supplying the needs of the affluent elderly while the *nonprofit, tax-exempt,* or *tax-favored* religiously sponsored groups might find a nobler work among the needier?

When that question was put to the profit-motivated developers of retirement communities they maintained a discreet silence. At the most they suggested that the building industry was well equipped to take care of the middle- to upper-income market, pay its full share of the tax load into local, state, and federal coffers, and still show a reasonable profit.

The replies from administrators of the nonprofit group varied slightly. But one Southern California administrator reacted so violently to the suggestion that his quote proved to be a revelation.

"It would be impossible," exclaimed the reverend gentleman, "for these church-sponsored homes to cater primarily to the indigent and the needy. It is difficult enough as it is! Read your newspaper! Every day the doctors announce that they are winning the war on one of the major diseases. These are the killing diseases. Take them away from us and how will we ever empty our rooms to make way for new life-care residents? How," he cried in genuine distress, "could we protect ourselves against a situation like this?"

In addition to the tax advantages and financing aids, many of these church-related nonprofit places enjoy several other advantages that help ensure them against the disastrous eventuality of total victory over the killing diseases. One such is the founder's fee. There are as many synonyms for this dollar-getting device as there are labels for the retirement homes' relationship to the parent organizations that inspire, sponsor, orient, initiate, institute, instigate, or motivate them.

Founder's fees are also called "admittance fees," "accommodation fees," "life lease fees," "occupancy fees," "membership fees," and occasionally they are called by their proper names, "advance gifts."

A fee by any other name is just as sweet to the nonprofit institution that receives it. In addition to being tax free, it may also be nonreturnable. In the event a senior resident should come into the home and find it difficult to adjust to this way of life, it is possible that a portion of the fee will be returned (within certain time limits) in which case a deduction of about 2 per cent per month is made for the total time of the resident's actual stay.

In those retirement homes where life-care also includes major medical care, very stringent physical examinations are generally mandatory before acceptance. Often these examinations are a requirement of the state welfare authorities also.

When queried about this physical requirement one administrator answered, *"It is very depressing for our well residents to spend their golden years among the infirm, the halt, and the lame. We feel in the end that we perform a finer Christian service for our residents if we reject those old people who are sick.*

"We know, of course, that a certain percentage of our well residents will become sick during their stay here. Naturally we will do all we are able to take care of them."

The simple truth seems to be that because of staff limitations only the well are considered good business risks. The ailing elderly, even though in many cases they may be able to afford the same level of medical care, simply must make other living arrangements. As one better rejectee put it, "My arthritis was kicking up when I applied so naturally they wouldn't touch me with a ten-foot pole. It was obvious from the minute I entered their doctor's office that it was going to be a 'heads we win, tails you lose' sort of a game."

Precautions are elaborately planned in these nonprofit, life-care retirement homes. In nearly all of them the entire founder's fee is kept by the home in the event a resident should die. Under this arrangement it is possible that an elderly person may pay up to $50,000 in founder's fees, live in the home for a few months, be stricken, and die—not an uncommon occurrence. In this event the home may keep not only the $50,-000 in its entirety but it also may resell or lease the living quarters. Said one administrator, "This is one of the few little edges we have in this game."

But this is not the only "edge" that may be employed in the game of nonprofit fiscal nest-feathering. In some places where life-care is provided for a flat fee based on actuarial tables, if the resident dies before having used up his projected rental and living expense money—paid in full in advance—the home may keep the unspent portion of that too.

Actually, very few outlive the actuarial tables as did the nonagenarian who rejoiced that each day of his life henceforth was "on the house." However, when a resident does manage to beat the law of averages he or she immediately becomes, for public relations purposes, a star boarder indeed!

The actuarial tables themselves are interesting. The multi-billion-dollar insurance industry has been built on various sets of experience or actuarial tables compiled over the years. This experience spans the decades from 1843 to 1954. It is always being updated—more quickly now with the advent of the computer. Most American insurance companies are now using the Commissioners 1958 Standard Ordinary Tables which show deaths per 1000 population in every age bracket from 1 year to 109 years in one column and expectation of life years for the same general span in a second column.

In this table the life expectancy of an "average" American at age sixty-five is 12.90 years. At age seventy it is 10.12 years and at age seventy-five it is 7.81 years.

One of the most difficult problems of research was to get access to the special actuarial tables used by the nonprofit, church-affiliated homes—"our little black books" they were often called.

With the exception of some tables issued by state welfare departments and consulted by the administrators of these homes, it was impossible in most instances to peruse even briefly the specially compiled tables upon which life-care charges were computed.

Finally, because of a genuine personal interest in the problem of retirement housing and care for members of our immediate family, it was possible to see a few specific figures that could be compared with the Commissioners Standard Ordinary Tables.

Invariably the nonprofit retirement homes' privately compiled tables were higher. If the sample is typical of most tables used by these places, then it could mean, of course, that life-care costs computed on them would run somewhat higher than those computed on the accepted insurance tables. When this possibility was voiced the replies were enlightening:

"We have found that the commissioners tables are unrealistic for us," said one manager who expressed the opinion held by most of those interviewed. "You see, when elderly persons come into one of our homes the really superior loving care we are able to give them has a tendency to prolong their lives by about four and a half years. We must take this added expense into account in order to stay solvent and continue our good work."

Another argument in defense of the private actuarial table went like this:

"The people who can afford to come to us are not average people. Because of their circumstances they have been able to afford the best medical care and a consistently good diet throughout most of their lives. Consequently they reach us in better condition and have a better chance to outlive the average life-expectancy projections. We must compensate for this."

Of those quoted no two of the private tables were identical. Some of them indicated longer life expectancies in the upper age groups by as much as five years. It was interesting to note however that in those nonprofit homes where supplementary commercial insurance plans were offered to the elderly there was apparently no reluctance on the part of the administrators to permit the insurance companies to use their own standard actuarial tables and to base their charges accordingly.

What these life-expectancy tables may mean to elderly residents in terms of dollars and cents can be illustrated in a general way by using figures obtained from one of the largest of the nonprofit, tax-favored retirement-home corporations licensed by the state of California.

According to their tables for age sixty-two—the minimum admittance age—a man has a life expectancy of 17.06 years and a woman's is 19.54 years. Averaging the two to bring them into a closer relationship to the Commissioners Standard Ordinary Tables for 1958 produces a figure of 18.30 years. The insurance companies using the C.S.O. tables show a life expectancy of only 14.78 years, a difference at age sixty-two of 3.52 years. (At age seventy, the difference was 5 years.)

Rounding it to 3.50 years this means that an average senior resident would pay about $3295 per year for three and a half years or $11,532.50 *more* by the private tables than if the rate were computed by the actuarial tables used by the majority of the major American life insurance companies, whose experience, one administrator suggested, had proved to be "undependable."

When advised of this one large West Coast underwriter of health insurance plans feigned indignation:

"I don't know what this world is coming to! One could hope that these good people would have considered it their Christian duty to warn us of our error in computing life expectancies."

Averages are broad guide lines at best and it is true that where actuarial tables are concerned the size of the group over which the risk is spread can affect the projections. However, there seems to be some valid reason for questioning the absolute accuracy of the contention that elderly persons tend to live longer in these upper-crust retirement homes because of the tender loving care they get—a claim made, incidentally, by all retirement homes contacted that cater to this socio-economic group.

First, any couple who could afford at age sixty-two to pay $142,780 for life-care—plus other continuing expenses not covered in the fee—must certainly have been able to afford as good food and medical care and as agreeable social surroundings *before* retirement as they may expect in a retirement home.

Second, it does not seem reasonable that the great life insurance companies of America would have overlooked the possibility of unusual longevity in a segment of the market in which lies one of their greatest potential volumes of underwriting.

Third, while it is true that the life expectancy of a child born in 1965 is considerably longer—on the average seventy years of life may be expected—it is also true that the smallest increase in life expectancy was found among those sixty-five and over.

In short, while there are more old people now, due to medical advances that have preserved more lives in the early and middle years, those who have presently survived to old age are living only a year or two longer on the average.

Women do have a slight advantage over men. These findings, noted in insurance research projects and confirmed by census studies and studies done in the Department of Health, Education and Welfare, are directly contrary to the contention of some of the nonprofit retirement homes that older people are showing a tendency to live *"significantly longer lives"* under their tender ministrations.

There are many variations of the life-care plan used by the nonprofit, retirement homes. One of the oldest methods is to require an applicant to agree to sign some or all of his worldly goods over to the organization in return for total care.

Generally there must be a minimum amount in such an estate to ensure basic financing, although in some church-oriented homes an elderly person will be admitted upon signing such a pledge regardless of the size of the estate. In such cases the home may also request that such a person agree to apply for outside charitable assistance from family and friends and from the proper welfare organizations. For instance, here are the requirements for admission to one such retirement home near Washington, D.C.:

The first is active membership in the church within that particular Conference for at least ten years prior to filing for application.[1] The applicant must also be in good physical and mental health.

If there are more than enough assets to provide care on a life-expectancy basis, the applicant is permitted to keep 50 per cent of any resources above the estimated cost of life-care.[2]

The costs are determined by the auditors each year and are revised according to the findings. If the applicant has less than the amount specified all resources are turned over to the home at the time of entrance.

Two per cent interest is paid on the amount turned in as long as such resources last. Then, when the applicant no longer has resources he may apply for Old Age Assistance under the Social Security Act.

If the applicant is ineligible for this assistance because of employed children, the home asks the children to contribute toward the care of the parent. The home states that all eligible applicants are admitted regardless of their financial condition and assures that each guest will receive the same care and services.

In the case of pensions and other income the home divides these with the guest. The amount allowed for purely personal

---

[1] A rare requirement.
[2] I.e., if the person's total estate is $100,000 and life-care is computed at $60,000, the person would be permitted to keep only $20,000 of the $40,000 excess. Presumably the home keeps the balance.

use will depend upon the total amount of the income. *Insurance policies are assigned to the home.*

If the cost of care eventually exceeds the amount contributed there is an understanding, made at time of entrance, that the guest will apply for other assistance that might be available, including Old Age Assistance. However, since Old Age Assistance does not cover the cost of care, according to the home, it is made clear that contributions must be relied upon from the churches in the form of offerings, annual maintenance subscriptions, and special gifts.

When asked what is given in return for agreeing to assign his worldly goods to the home the applicant is reassured in the brochure that he will receive "Christian love and concern —room, board, health-care in the infirmary—in short all needs are provided for so that a resident is able to enjoy a life free from material worries."

In the event a resident should not like this mode of living after entering the home all money will be refunded except what has actually been used for his care.

Since there is no monthly charge made at this particular retirement home the life-care charges probably require a sizable estate if the applicant expects to keep any of the allowed 50 per cent above the estimated life-care costs.

In a number of the largest of these luxury retirement homes an applicant is required to submit a financial statement.

If the minimum required income (generally $250 a month) does not come from "blue chip" investments or pensions it may be necessary for members of the applicant's immediate family to cosign the contract. Remittances from children or other relatives and friends are not considered "safe" sources of income.

As with so many of these life-care, nonprofit, tax-favored institutions, despite substantial advantages under law, there is no reticence about asking residents to apply for other benefits supplied wholly or in part by the taxpayers. Certainly there is nothing wrong with this request if a retirement home

is actually carrying a maximum burden of needy elderly charity cases. All in all, however, there would seem to be very little
madness in their method.

Except for those life-care institutions where everything is
paid for in a lump sum—in advance—the minimum annual income needed for a couple to enjoy the blessings of most of
these church-sponsored, tax-favored, nonprofit retirement
homes is approximately $7000—or about $4500 more annually
than the median money income for the head of a family of two
at age sixty-five and over as given in the U. S. Census Bureau
consumer income figure.

This median figure is one of those averages again and must
be reckoned as such. But the Bureau of Labor Statistics did
an in-depth survey of living costs for such a couple in the
principal cities and came up with an average income of $3010
as the minimum needed annually for an adequate level of
living.

The one point that emerges quite clearly in any investigation
of retirement living is that the principal effort of both profit-
motivated and nonprofit developers is being concentrated in
income brackets well above the median income figure that, in
itself, is well above the income bracket in which exists most of
the need for decent surroundings.

The questions being asked most frequently now are ones
that cannot make for complacency in the ranks of those tax-
favored, nonprofit retirement developers who are virtually
dominating the field. They are:

"Why should taxpayers have to bear any portion of the expense of operating these places for seniors of ample means
who are able to take care of themselves when nearly ten million
needy elders must rely on relatives or relief in order to manage
a very minimal existence?" And: "If fully tax-burdened profit-
motivated operators can compete for the same lucrative market
and do it successfully on the basis of comparable services and
facilities, then why can't nonprofit places tighten up management procedures and do the same?"

There is some evidence that they can if they want to. Some truly charitable organizations do operate with great efficiency and pass the advantages along to the elderly in lower costs.

In Miami Beach, Florida, at the President Madison Hotel operated for senior citizens by Four Freedoms, Inc., a non-profit, union-sponsored organization, accommodations complete with all meals and recreation but without major medical insurance are $185 a month per person or $250 for two persons. *There are no other mandatory fees.* There is an optional Blue Cross-Blue Shield medical-surgical insurance program available to residents that is generally considered to rate with the best protection of its kind in the country today.

The $185 per month per person for accommodations and all meals compares very favorably with the profit-motivated Blackstone Hotel just down the street in Miami and with the profit-motivated Roosevelt in Washington, D.C. The same is true of the two-person charges.

Comparable accommodations in several nonprofit, tax-favored retirement facilities averaged about $50 a month more. And in addition, a substantial founder's fee was mandatory. This ranged from $7000 to $13,500 payable in advance. There were also other charges, application fees (non-returnable), registration fees, processing fees, and so on. These often ran to more than $100 per person. *In some instances these nonreturnable fees are charged simply for the privilege of applying for admission.*

If one may assume about the same general tax advantages for both union-motivated and church-motivated facilities of comparable size and quality, then it would appear that the church-motivated device, the founder's fee, a device not used by the principal union-motivated facilities, may be in the nature of "gravy" on the meat and potatoes expenses of financing since the Four Freedoms union group, for instance, is able, without such an advantage, to acquire new and very valuable real estate and build the most modern retirement facilities in several major American cities including Miami, Seattle, Detroit, Philadelphia, Pittsburgh, San Francisco, Los Angeles, Boston, New York, and Baltimore. Also, this is being accomplished without any other comparable lump-sum payment in advance.

In fairness to the church-sponsored groups it should be noted that some of them do operate excellent retirement homes with nursing or infirmary facilities and modern hospitals in connection with their living facilities. Often their charges do include part of and sometimes all of the medical and nursing care a resident may need. But in a number of places, such vital nursing care could be had only after paying an additional charge. The charges vary from $250 to $750 monthly.

It should be remembered, however, that in comparable profit-motivated retirement facilities where only minor medical and dispensary care is available, it is possible to secure standard health insurance, usually with a deductible feature,[3] that also will meet most major medical expenses. The higher the deductible the greater the benefits.

A number of the church-motivated people argue that they take unusual risks in providing for medical care in their life-care payments. But it would seem that they do a great deal to minimize such risks also. As has been pointed out, many of them require applicants to present a detailed physical report made out by their own personal physicians. Then, before final acceptance, the applicant must also submit to another thorough physical examination given by the retirement home's medical staff. These precautions are somewhat more elaborate than those taken by the average life insurance company these days.

It is not unusual for the life-care contracts to place limitations on liability under their own medical plans. Several of those contacted advise their life-care residents to invest in *additional insurance* to cover certain contingencies. Only a very small number of life-care homes appear to make any effort to include dentistry, podiatry, and the care of ears and eyes in their coverage.

[3] The patient pays the first $100 to $500 of accrued expenses.

Several of the life-care homes contacted had certain very strict rules requiring the use of their own doctors in case of serious illness. Their staff physicians' opinions exert great influence over management's policy and may determine how long a resident should be hospitalized and the extent of any nursing care.

Recently some church-associated, tax-favored, nonprofit retirement homes have been taking still further precautions to protect their funds by writing into their contracts a 5 per cent annual cost of living increase clause. Some of the clauses limit the increase to a total of 25 per cent.

In certain of the life-care places if a specialist is deemed necessary it is at the patient's expense. Also, if the patient should not want the staff doctor he must pay additionally for a doctor of his own choice. This also applies to a preferred hospital, clinic, or nursing home.

Residents have expressed concern about this feature, saying that if the best "heart man" or "cancer specialist" happens to be in another city and was urgently needed a great additional expense would be sustained. The alternative would be to make-do with the care at hand.

In all of these comparisons the central question remains the same: Are the tax advantages enjoyed by the majority of the nonprofit retirement homes justifiable when for approximately the same money and often for less the profit-motivated organizations are able to provide the same services and still pay their share of the economy's upkeep?

The government itself has implemented these advantages to the nonprofit organizations, both in the Bureau of Internal Revenue with tax exemptions under certain conditions and in the Federal Housing Administration under its various sections, but most particularly under its very active Section 231.

Sidney Woolner, Commissioner of the Communities Facilities Administration of the Housing and Home Finance Agency, the parent organization, said in a paper prepared for the Institute on Non-Profit Independent Housing as a Living

Environment for Older People held in Glenwood Springs, Colorado, in July 1962, "The FHA program has an advantage of being highly flexible, even though for the most part it concentrates on housing for persons who are reasonably well-off."

Among the increasing number of church officials who are genuinely concerned about the tendency of some of the church-related, nonprofit, tax-exempt retirement facilities to liberalize the interpretation of charity to selfish ends and to cater almost entirely to the affluent elderly, one of the most thoughtful and outspoken is the Reverend Lawrence M. Upton, Secretary for Services to the Aging of the United Church Board for Homeland Ministries in New York City.

Speaking at Glenwood Springs, Colorado, before the Institute on Non-Profit Independent Housing as a Living Environment for Older People, this forward-looking church executive jarred the complacency of some of this fraternity while discussing the characteristics and responsibilities of sponsorship of these nonprofit retirement homes.

The occasion was a meeting of the Leadership Institute Series sponsored by the National Council on the Aging and co-sponsored by the remarkable Metropolitan Denver Conference of Non-Profit Housing for the Aging, a part of the Metropolitan Council for Community Services in Denver.

The Reverend Lawrence Upton said, in part:

I think there can be no question at all that most of the projects which have been created within the last decade are far beyond the means of any but a small minority of our elderly population. I am not suggesting, hereby, that people who are well-to-do do not need facilities and protective services that are being provided. But I have no reluctance in saying that most of the projects are too expansive and too expensive for a large constituency of elderly people who, with the assistance of the federal programs, could and should be served.

Most of the sponsors related to religious bodies have created projects for the luxury and semi-luxury class alone. This is not only true in evaluating the per-unit cost of most of the projects, but also, and perhaps even more strikingly, it is true when one evaluates the methods of financing. Nearly all of the projects require a substantial Founder's Fee or life-tenancy fee, which can range from perhaps $3,500 at the lower limits to $50,000.

The Reverend Secretary continued on the subject of financing:

Prior to the availability of long-term, long-interest financing, the only way in which a project for elderly people could be created was either by using private philanthropy or by exacting a substantial sum of money from the person entering the project. . . .

Predominately church bodies have continued this method of financing even though they are now eligible for and may avail themselves of long-term, low-interest financing. . . .

These life-tenancy fees are no longer necessary, and they are an embarrassment to the sponsor because of the surplus capital which builds up over the years.[4] . . .

Sometimes this policy is justified on the Robin Hood theory—"we take from the rich to support the poor"— although it is rather difficult to find very many instances where the "poor" have been served. . . .

Establishments which have been in existence for several years can point with questionable pride to the surplus funds which they have in their accounts, and one frequently hears glib comments about the establishment's ability, at some future time, to serve those who are less prosperous. Many sponsors have ignored completely the gross unfairness involved in charging a person with a life-expectancy of, say, five years the same life-tenancy fee that it charges a person with a life-expectancy of, for instance, twenty years.

[4] Authors' italics.

After going over some figures to prove the above assertion, the Reverend Lawrence Upton continued:

It is my conviction that unless and until the sponsors orient their programs to people of more modest financial resources, until they reduce the expansiveness and expensiveness in design, and until they begin to require rigid economies in the management of these facilities, the sponsors are in danger of being utterly unmindful of the needs of a significant fraction of our elderly people.

Lawrence Upton then turned his attention to another aspect of these church-sponsored, nonprofit, tax-exempt retirement homes.

The upper middle class orientation of most boards of directors is also reflected in the social policies in the management of the projects. Very few of the sponsors related to religious bodies have given more than passing recognition to the social value of keeping elderly people active so long as possible in caring for their own life patterns. Most sponsors would feel that they are degrading their project if any of the residents were to be employed on the staff of the establishment. Most of the projects which have provided apartments with kitchenettes either require all of the occupants to eat at the common dining facility or they give no concession to those who prefer to cook for themselves. Thus a woman who has cooked successfully for sixty years has to be provided with occupational therapy, much of which is contrived activity, because she is either not permitted to or not encouraged to do that which for most of her life has been a significant activity in daily routine.

Although Lawrence Upton finds much good being done in many of the church-related retirement homes, he does seem to confirm in the following observation another tendency noted elsewhere in these pages.

This upper bourgeois orientation is further manifested

in the ethnic, creedal and racial exclusiveness in nearly all of our existing projects for elderly people.

The following year the Reverend Lawrence Upton was again expressing his concern before the delegates to the new Housing Institute sponsored by the National Council on the Aging and co-sponsored by the San Francisco Program for the Aging of the United Community Fund of that city. Speaking at Pacific Grove in September 1963, Lawrence Upton said in part:

One of the most serious problems of the life-tenancy fee system is that it discourages practical economies which are necessary in providing facilities for the low and moderate income elderly.

A non-profit sponsor anticipating hundreds of thousands, or even a million dollars or more in Founder's Fees has a built-in tendency to extravagance in design. . . . This is not uncommon in facilities created under the life-tenancy fee system of financing. Inescapably, the occupants of such a facility must pay very, very high rents for their living accommodations.

And then, on the subject of the church-sponsored retirement facilities vulnerability, he added this:

The next problem in the life-tenancy fee type of financing is that it is *eroding our tax position*. As you know in Oregon and California we have had tax cases go through litigation clear to the Supreme Court. In both states the homes involved have large Founder's Fees. These tax cases have subjected all (tax-exempt) facilities for the elderly to a fresh scrutiny in various states of the nation.

Charity came in for a little scrutiny too, as the Reverend Lawrence Upton continued:

The next issue involves the ability of the home to provide charitable services. Founder's Fees paid by the first, second or third generation of occupants should enable a home to provide substantial charitable services. . . . I claim that the federal programs which provide 100%

financing will enable the non-profit sponsor to provide some charitable service as soon as the project is fully occupied. This is true because all of the programs require that the financing projections must allow for a five to seven percent vacancy.

There seems to be a tendency to use Founder's Fee funds for other purposes than to enable the facilities to admit tenants who can afford only rentals and maintenance costs, or who may require charitable services. In some instances non-profit sponsors have delayed extension of charitable services long after the period when the project is fully occupied, solvent and able to carry the cost of such services. . . . (Authors' italics)

These statements must surely imply an urgent need for an answer to the question of how much longer the taxpayers can assume the burden of public housing, Social Security, and some form of medical care for the rapidly increasing senior segment of the population without demanding that tax-favored, nonprofit institutions catering to the affluent elderly reorient themselves, as their own thoughtful leaders caution them to, and begin carrying their fair share of the total burden.

Until this question is officially raised it may be expected that these organizations will go right on acquiring choice urban real estate and building the most expensive and expansive modern facilities and adding to their already immense capital wealth, all in the name of offering tender loving care with a considerable degree of luxury to those affluent senior citizens who can afford it and who demand it because for years it has been their accustomed way of life.

13

AS IT IS IN HEAVEN

What do the residents of these church-inspired, nonprofit retirement homes think about this way of life? As might be expected, most of those who can afford the tariff think it is quite literally "heaven on earth."

This unusually appropriate metaphor was used by another reverend gentleman who administers a famous resort hotel turned nonprofit retirement home. "At this place," he said, not without a touch of humor, "we are so beautifully endowed by nature with heaven on earth that our seniors don't seem to want to go on!"

This administrator was speaking of what he called "the tendency of many of our elderly residents to outlive their life-expectancy projections." This was simply a repetition of a point of view concerning the alleged tendency that has been noted by other such administrators. It is being "viewed with alarm" in administrative circles in many of the more elaborate life-care homes.

There seems to be some reason to suspect, however, that the reverend gentlemen are less concerned with the lengthening lives of their older residents—a phenomenon that contradicts the statements of government and insurance-company observers—than they are with rising costs in our inflation-prone economy. After all, if a life-care retirement home contracts with a resident to pay room, board, and some if not all medical expenses there is a very real possibility that rising costs could put the squeeze on budgets if management had not allowed sufficient cost of living increases in the prices in the first place.

The solution to this possible pinch in the tax-free pocket-book seems to be a general trend away from the fixed-fee, life-care charges in favor of a founder's fee plus a monthly charge for the usual services with the further provision written into the agreement that the monthly charge may be increased by certain increments and at stated intervals if the auditors indicate such a move is necessary. Here again the retired person with a fixed income is in a trap.

It is interesting to note that the law in California and in other states has defined these nonprofit, church-inspired retirement homes as charitable institutions. Nothing is said in these definitions that would identify them with an industry. But apparently in the fierce competition to serve this wealthy and growing segment of our society these places operating under the auspices of churches and other organizations are finding that in certain fundamental respects there is little difference between their concept of charity and the open conflict of the market place.

Competitively, these places are not without certain advantages other than lenient taxation. Many of them are located on some of the most desirable and therefore valuable real estate in the nation. Certainly if there is a heaven on earth in the sense of physical setting the management of one luxurious home is not amiss in describing it as such, sitting as it does on a promontory overlooking a rock-bound crescent of sandy bathing beach that curves to meet the beautiful expanse of the Pacific. The appointments are no less lovely than the location.

While waiting in the lounge to visit with the administrator we were taken in tow by a charming lady who introduced herself as Mrs. Dennis. For two and a half years she and her husband have lived in the home after having given up a luxurious residence in a fashionable suburb of Los Angeles, California.

The couple travel when possible. They had just returned

from an extended visit to the South Pacific, where they had been able to pursue their hobby of taking color photographs. They call themselves amateurs despite the fact that they had studied color photography with some outstanding professionals. Mr. and Mrs. Dennis were preparing to give the residents a "magic lantern" tour of the islands through the medium of their remarkable slides.

When asked how they liked life at the retirement resort after so many years of living in their own elegant home, Mrs. Dennis replied for both by saying, "It is wonderful! Simply wonderful! Of course our own home was lovely, too, but we are so happy now not to have the responsibility of running a big place. And we do enjoy the peace of mind of being able to do as we please now, secure in the knowledge that everything is paid for and taken care of for the rest of our lives. It is wonderful, I can assure you!"

Another happy couple who have been completely captivated by church-sponsored, luxurious retirement living in the Monterey Bay area in northern California is Mr. and Mrs. Stanton Lewis. Mr. Lewis had retired as an executive of one of the large utility companies on the Pacific coast. His point of view on retirement at age sixty-five was interesting because it seemed to run counter to the usual opinions. He said, "I think retirement for us businessmen at age sixty-five is right and proper because then we avoid the problems of jealousies on the part of men we work with who may not be equally effective at that same age. If we all retire at the same age we spare ourselves and others much possible trouble and also make room at the top for young men who deserve a chance to prove themselves."

Most retired men were reluctant to admit that. They seemed to feel that the companies would have been much better off if they had kept on availing themselves of their senior employees' experience until the elders were no longer able to keep up. Most of them, at least at the outset of their retirement, wore their resentment like a dark mantle. Unlike their wives, they paid begrudging compliments to their luxurious retirement surroundings.

Mrs. Lewis said, "I am delighted to be able to share Stan now. We have both taken up golf and it is a whole new way of life for us! You see," she explained, "I was never an enthusiastic cook and housekeeper so having all of this done for me is a sheer luxury."

On the subject of handing over the bulk of their estate in return for life-care Mrs. Lewis made this observation:

"We feel we could leave our children no better legacy than not to burden them with us in our old age and to have them know that we are doing exactly what we desire."

Mr. Lewis did confess that at first he missed some of his old civic duties. "I worried a little," he said. "I missed the Chamber of Commerce and the service club work. But now I'm so busy here that I'm surprised they haven't put me on the payroll."

Between his golf and his duties as president of the residents' committee, which plans and administers all of the social and recreational activities, Stan Lewis need never worry about time lying heavily on his hands. Just the work of writing the constitution and bylaws of the group was a matter of some weeks. Parenthetically it should be noted that Stan Lewis' industry and skill at such documents undoubtedly saved the retirement home many hundreds of dollars in legal fees.

Mr. and Mrs. Lewis add variety to their comfortable retirement by playing golf on as many courses as possible in the Carmel-Monterey-Pacific Grove area. That means they have a wide choice of some of the best courses in the country including the world-famous courses at Pebble Beach where Bing Crosby's annual tournaments are held.

Anyone seeking to emulate the Lewises' routine had better make certain that an ample sum is set aside over and above life-care and the additional health insurance that the retirement home recommends (to take care of *unusual* medical emergencies) because even on a good public course, golf is no longer an inexpensive pastime.

Another point of view was voiced by a delightful lady in her seventies who had successfully run an importing company for many years:

"The best thing we can leave our children is the knowledge that we will never be a burden to them."

Commenting on the effect of life-care living on the elderly retirees she had this to say: "I have seen the greatest change in people since they've been here. Many of them came here all withdrawn. And then all of a sudden they blossomed out . . . and in such a short time too!"

When asked why she thought this change came over them she replied, "Old houses become a burden. Not only is the up-keep difficult and the expense greater but they are filled with memories that can be painful. Once left behind, those burdens are lifted and forgotten and it is easy to brighten up."

Two New York schoolteachers—a husband and wife—with two separate retirement incomes gave up their home on Long Island and their mountain summer place in an adjoining state. They systematically traveled to all of the principal retirement homes and chose one not far from San Francisco in a beautiful mountain valley. They called this church-motivated place "a Godsend"!

"Most of the places we saw took better care of their lawns than their residents," said the husband. "But not here! To us this seems like perpetual spring. It is very much like our eastern mountains—but never cold—and always green."

This couple had little difficulty in adjusting to this sort of life-care retirement.

"Teachers make the transition easily, we feel, because of our long summer vacations and our sabbaticals," they said. When asked their opinion about handing over the bulk of their estate to the home for life-care they replied, "We feel it is wrong to subsidize our children."

It is difficult to tell just how much of this general negative attitude toward estates for children is actually altruistic. No matter where they were interviewed in the United States this same attitude was prevalent among the relatively affluent couples who had retired.

One sociologist feels that there may be an element of rationalization present. "These older couples may feel a bit guilty about taking all of their savings and using them for a lifetime vacation. Hence they may feel the need to justify what could be a selfish act by rationalizing it as an action taken for the good of their children—a sort of 'this spanking hurts me more than it hurts you' attitude."

One woman who asked that her name not be used and who had some second thoughts about life-care payments in one of the "hand-over-all-your-worldly-goods" retirement homes not far from New York said this:

"I paid everything I had. And then when I was in there I started thinking and changed my mind. I was happy to let them keep the money for my board for three months and the charge they made for processing my papers.

"At first I thought it was the most sensible solution to my problem—not to be a burden to my children and to be surrounded by those of my own age and income level.

"But very soon I began to feel like I was being poured into a mold—and being forced to pay a small fortune for the privilege. Not only did they want absolutely everything but they demanded a pledge from my two boys that they would make cash contributions if illness used up the $70,000 and more that I'd paid. I also had to sign an agreement that I would apply for public aid in that event too. Suddenly I felt as though I were being drained of all my money, my independence, and my self-respect too. It was too much! I just wanted out!

"My sons have reinvested the returned money for me now and have bought me what seems to be a good health insurance policy. Barring some sort of disastrous illness I should be all right without being any more of a burden on them than I would have been in that dreadful place where they would have had to hand me charity anyway."

She reflected briefly, then added: "I think the whole thing is—sacrilegious."

Another point of view on this "heaven on earth" type of retirement living came from a nonagenarian who has been able to observe his fellow human beings with an understanding heart for three quarters of a century. Alert and interested, Harry Morrison slapped the arm of his favorite chair.

"Maybe I'd change my tune if I didn't have a loving family around me. But I don't think so! I can't imagine anything on earth that would make a man into a vegetable faster than going into the same dining room in the same place with the same people—sitting in the same chair on the same terrace—playing the same card games with the same people—talking over the same ailments . . ."

He grimaced, then continued. "That is not for thinking human beings. That is for sheep! What are they going to do when they've put together the last jigsaw puzzle?" he demanded. "I have visited friends in those places—expensive places. They are all put away in the dead file. They are not living anymore. They are in sandboxes for the senile. They are playing patty-cake . . . doing stupid things to keep from thinking about death. If you want to keep from thinking about death you must think about life. You must stay interested in the world . . . find ways to be useful to people."

Harry Morrison's point of view is shared by other rugged individualists. Generally such men are professionals of one sort or another. They are emphatic, often amusing. But what they may forget is this: Not everyone has a profession that he can pursue independently for as long as he wishes or for as long as he is physically able.

Dr. Joseph Peck advocates communities for the aged called "Opportunity Villages," where all of the retired in this country can live and continue to pursue their life works on a limited basis for limited pay in order to impart to each a sense of continuing usefulness.

But what Dr. Peck would do, really, is to substitute one kind of retirement community for another—and a far less practical one. Actually, if they wish to, professional men can continue to pursue their professions in a very satisfying manner in most of the retirement communities in the country today. They must, of course, secure the necessary state licenses. Admittedly there are fewer such opportunities for the retired businessman who was in sales or production or engineering or planning. These men are given some substitutes for their former responsibilities in such committee work as Stanton Lewis has undertaken or in the activities of Albert E. Woolen at Kern City. Mr. Woolen, who had always been close to the civic activities and affairs of his home town, looked forward to the inactivity of retirement with some misgivings.

"But I needn't have worried," he said, pointing to a stack of official-looking papers on his writing desk. "It seems they still want me on the county committee on school district organization, and I've already served for two years on the Kern City Council that manages the activities of this community. I'm as busy now as I want to be."

Mr. Woolen also has become an expert breeder of fancy orchids and his greenhouse in the back yard of his pleasant home in Kern City is a wonderland of rare blossoms.

So it would seem that "one man's heaven is another man's hell" in the world of retirement living also. But these two states of being (or mind) have varying levels and in the retirement communities under discussion the levels are all fairly high. They are enjoyed or endured by retired persons whose means are sufficient to provide them with more than average comfort and with a relatively high degree of security, at least for their active years.

It is difficult to get most retirees to confide the exact state of their personal finances. But the impression, after many interviews, was that there are more than a few of those enjoying a degree of comfort, if not luxury, in their retired years who may be able to pay for medical expenses now but who, like Z.K. in Chapter 1, may have to pray for the money later—if catastrophic illness visits them and capital funds are depleted.

It is in protecting against this unhappy exigency that some of the life-care places perform a commendable service. The problem, of course, is that the taxpayer is being made, however indirectly, to bear a share of the burden of maintaining these relatively affluent elderly life-care residents in comfort, but it may be too that he will be forced to face the reality of having his tax burden still further increased to care for some of those who have assumed obligations in profit-motivated retirement places and then have found that illness has wiped out their assets and obliged them to seek public assistance. This is no theoretical possibility; catastrophic illness has already forced repossession in some places.

Nobody can say yet how much of a problem this may grow to be with fixed incomes attempting to cover rising costs. Builders are inclined to pooh-pooh the idea. "A man with a net worth of $125,000 is a good credit risk!" they say. And still, a score of retired persons were found whose assets had equaled that amount at age sixty-five but who had been impoverished at seventy-five by protracted illnesses against which their insurance protection had been inadequate or non-existent. Obviously the danger of this eventuality is potentially greater in those luxurious profit-motivated retirement facilities where the purchaser is required to obligate himself for long periods without the privilege of paying up and taking clear title. He may realize a modest profit, but his equity is almost certain to be small in the event of a resale.

Against this disadvantage, of course, is the very great advantage of relatively small down payments and very modest monthly payments, both of which are attractive, especially to those retirees who wish to enjoy caviar living on corned-beef budgets. For many of them the powerful pull of the *money magnets* makes the risk seem justifiable.

But theoretical though such a risk may presently be to the developers, there is nothing theoretical about the statement that a person who runs out of money in one of the profit-motivated retirement cities also runs out of luck—usually under particularly devastating circumstances.

Though the incidence did not seem high, there were a number of "For Sale" signs to be seen in the several Sun Cities visited. Various reasons were given for putting these dwellings back on the market. The full facts were not always available from management. But neighbors were not so reticent.

"The house next door is in pretty bad shape," said a resident of Kern City, "because the couple who bought it found they couldn't cut the mustard with the payments. He got ill and it was too much for them to handle with just Social Security."

In several other instances elsewhere it was found that retirees had settled for substantial losses in order to be free of the burden of long mortgages after an unexpected illness struck.

Admittedly this can and does occur in *any* housing development. But, in reckoning the odds, a retiree who is about to obligate himself for from twenty-five to forty years under a mortgage should bear in mind that his chances of succumbing to a catastrophic illness are far greater at retirement age and beyond than those of a young family just starting out who may be tempted to assume a similar obligation.

It was pointed out that this sort of emergency generally does not arise in the church-motivated, nonprofit retirement places. But the fact that evictions do not usually occur in such places does not seem to be reason enough to justify all of the special privileges they may take advantage of in providing for the elderly who feel they can afford a relatively carefree paid-up retirement.

Heaven on earth it may well be for those residents. But as the elderly segment of our society increases, those who will not be able to provide for themselves will surely create a veritable hell on earth both for the welfare authorities and for the taxpayer. The profit-motivated retirement communities cannot be expected to provide any extensive facilities for charitable care though some of them do, voluntarily, and the church-motivated, nonprofit places upon whom charitable responsibility does devolve under state laws can be expected to keep such cases to an absolute minimum until costly mortgages are amortized and until new acquisitions of real estate and new facilities are securely within their grasp.

Many church-motivated retirement places have been alerted by state tax officials, by their own legal advisers, and by their own administrators. They have been warned that a day of reckoning may be coming in the matter of deferring a maximum effort to serve the needy.

No word in the English language has been so loosely interpreted as the word, "charity." Lawyers defending certain nonprofit interests have even managed to win suits on the strength of their ambiguous definitions of the word.

In the days before certain special interests were permitted the advantages of tax forgiveness, charity was a forthright word with a plain and obvious meaning. As a single word it was the ultimate distillation of the spirit of the Golden Rule. It meant, simply, the act of helping those who were no longer able to help themselves.

In California the State Supreme Court broadened that definition. It judged charity to mean considerably more than alms to the needy, which was the clear definition under the Elizabethan concept of English law.

In one case in California the word charity implied the performance of its classic function, "including the relief of poverty but also the advancement of religion, the promotion of health, governmental or municipal purposes and other purposes the acknowledgment of which is beneficial to mankind."

Under a section headed "Comment" was a further elaboration:

> The general scope of charitable purposes is indicated in the preamble to the statute of charitable uses. (43 Elizabeth 1–1601)
> The common element of all charitable purposes is that they are defined to accept objects which are beneficial to

the community. The purpose is charitable if its accomplishment is of such social interest to the community to justify permitting the property to be devoted to the purpose in perpetuity.

In another case it was found that the "relief of poverty is not a condition of charitable assistance. . . . The concept of charity is not confined to the relief of the needy and destitute, for aged people require care and attention apart from financial assistance and the supplying of this care and attention is as much a charitable and benevolent purpose as the relief of their financial wants."

It was further held that "any person, the rich, as well as the poor, may fall sick or be injured or wounded and become a fit subject for charity. (As defined in St. Luke, Chapter Ten, verses 30–37.)

"It seems clear that a home for the aged which caters to wealthy persons and furnishes them those services and care needed by the old and the infirm, rich or poor, does not cease to be a charitable institution so long as its charges do not yield more than the actual costs of operation."

When that decision became the precedent for California law it was not surprising that a number of charitably inclined nonprofit, tax-exempt groups hastened to follow the injunction of Jesus to emulate the Good Samaritan.

It is difficult to get dependable figures on the extent to which they went forth and did likewise. But in a paper on federal, state, and local tax laws as they affect housing for the elderly, read before the members of the N.C.O.A.'s *Institute on Providing a Living Environment for Older People with Low and Lower-middle Incomes at a Price They Can Afford to Pay* at Asilomar, Pacific Grove, California, in September of 1963 it was stated that "after this decision a committee was appointed by the California Legislature to consider the problem of tax exemption.

"In their study, it was pointed out that the top twelve homes in California have an assessed valuation in excess of ten million dollars and, conservatively, taxes for these institutions would run to almost one million dollars a year."

Since that time it is estimated that in California alone at least another dozen such church-oriented, nonprofit, tax-favored or -exempted charitable homes have opened their doors or have announced construction.

It does not take a computer to see just how sweet charity may be for those who wish to make catering to the affluent elderly their primary effort—or, inversely, just how sour its taste may well become in the mouths of overburdened taxpayers whose own improved property is being assessed at higher and higher rates each year while these especially favored organizations continue to earmark tax-free reserves or credit for still more and more expansion of their prime real estate holdings.

A burdened, unprivileged taxpayer cannot be expected to look with favor upon a privileged group whose concept of charitable work encompasses mainly the providing of comfortable, even luxurious, living for a segment of our elderly population many of whose members quite probably can afford to winter in the South of France until their new tax-free retirement quarters are ready!

In Chicago a former member of the clergy who had given up his calling for private business remarked, "Most of these church-inspired retirement homes are connected to the parent organization by a sort of *"unbiblical cord"* through which it is possible for surplus money to flow. Profits do not necessarily have to be labeled as such, you know."

14

"THAR'S GOLD IN THEM THAR ILLS!"

Back in 1900 our senior citizen population was relatively small. There were only 3 million persons over sixty-five years of age in the United States.

Two decades later, in 1920, the figure had risen to 5 million. In 1940 our senior population had increased to 9 million. By 1960 it had grown to 16.5 million. In 1965 it numbers approximately 18.5 million and by 1980 it will number in excess of 24.4 million.

The projections go on to the year 2000, when it is expected our senior population will approach 35 million—an increase of tenfold in the twentieth century.

Since the turn of the century profound changes have been taking place in the status and in the attitude of the American senior citizen. His position in our society has changed radically.

In order to understand something of the profound psychological effect this changed status has had on him it is necessary to understand something of the economic upheavals that have caused it.

In 1900 the majority of American families, like those in most of Europe, still sheltered three generations under one roof. As the task of breadwinning passed from father to son, and son and wife began raising their own new generation of children, the older folks readjusted themselves to lesser space in the same houses.

"I think the kids ought to have the big bedroom now," was a familiar phrase. And so was, "I think the baby ought to be born in the same room his mother [or father] was born in."

An average American home then was a citadel of security. In the family there was continuity of purpose and effort. Families often worked for generations in the same trades and industries and located in the same areas.

But when the American version of the industrial revolution began to expand and complicate our economy by multiplying both the amounts and varieties of goods and services, we began to change the traditional pioneer economic and social patterns that had been established soon after Jamestown and Salem.

Only on the farms did the pattern persist to any extent. But after World War I, even that traditional stronghold began to crumble. The change was reflected in a number of ways, but few popular explanations were as clearly stated as the one embodied in the great hit song of 1919, "How Ya Gonna Keep 'Em Down on the Farm?" ("After they've seen Paree . . .").

The doughboys who returned were restless. Marriages made in haste as Johnny got his gun and took it "Over There" on the run began to falter, and a far-reaching new trend was begun in our society.

Years passed and middle-aged parents, left behind in the old three-generation homes, became elderly. The younger Americans were carried along to new centers of opportunity on the rising tide of our expanding economy. Then came the ebb during the recession after World War I and during the Great Depression of the thirties, which preceded World War II.

The process was repeated again during and after World War II until the old three-generation American home was virtually a thing of the past, outmoded, unhandy, too often left in what had become the least desirable residential districts of the expanding communities.

Two generations of the elderly were left with the most critical problems. In the majority of cases they lacked adequate means or the understanding to cope with them. One of the most important discoveries the sociologists needed to make was the foregoing. They had been thinking in terms of one generation of elderly Americans when, in fact, there were, and still are and always will be, *two distinct age groups with separate and special needs.* For, as we said earlier, today in America *one out of three* of the children who left the old three-generation family home forty years ago has a living relative over eighty years of age! That means these second-generation children themselves are now senior citizens past sixty.

Too often now there is a pathetic reunion of these two generations taking place because of a new mutual need, the final chapter in the long story of *inter*dependence that had kept them together under the same roof more than a half century earlier.

These aging Americans face many problems. But the greatest is the problem of finding the money to pay for the increasing incidence of serious illness that is the lot of most elderly persons. This problem and those irrevocably related to it are among the cruelest teeth in The Retirement Trap.

Some idea of the probabilities that face most elderly Americans may be had from the following figures:

The average senior at age sixty-five and older is ill five weeks out of the year.

Two of those weeks will be spent in bed and will necessitate care by a second person.

One out of six will go to the hospital and spend two weeks there.

Of the 18.7 million elderly, 12 million will suffer from one chronic ailment that limits their activities; 1.25 million of them are invalids.

900,000 are in institutions and will probably remain there for the duration of their lives.

For the one out of six elderly persons who go to the hospital each year the average charge will be $525. This will not include doctors' fees, nursing fees, and expensive diagnostic and treatment services.

The last Consumer Price Index available prior to publication indicates that all of our expenses in the United States have risen by 26 per cent. But of special interest to the elderly is the figure indicating that doctors' fees have risen by 47 per cent! *And hospital daily charges are up 150 per cent.*

For the affluent elderly these figures indicate an alarming but not necessarily a critical problem. But for the masses of elderly, 85 per cent of whom are unemployed and must live on or below the median income level—and on fixed incomes—these rising costs spell hardship and disaster.

It is not the purpose of this book to debate at length the merits of private insurance and medical care versus Social Security and compulsory Medicare. But with our elderly population increasing at the rate of a thousand persons a day, of which those needing financial assistance number some 100,000 each year, it must be evident even to the most myopic optimist that our society faces a tremendous problem if it is going to fulfill the promise of dignity and freedom from want that we are told is every American's birthright.

It must be obvious also that some form of mass, low-cost health insurance is now an absolute necessity.

When President John Kennedy delivered to the first session of the Eighty-eighth Congress his message on the elderly citizens of our nation and asked our lawmakers to give earnest consideration to the Medicare plan he advanced in considerable detail, the private health insurance underwriters of the nation hastened to have still another look at their businesses. The purpose was to see whether or not it was economically feasible for them to relieve some of the pressure through new plans for the aged and thereby avoid the worrisome prospect of having to compete for business with the federal government.

Out of this re-evaluation came a number of new health insurance plans designed specifically for those sixty-five and over with moderate incomes. It was a hopeful step toward broadening the base of medical and surgical coverage.

But insurance companies, like gamblers, base their multi-billion-dollar businesses upon the law of probabilities. And that immutable law dictated that certain precautions were economic necessities if the companies were to continue in business, make profits, and pay dividends to the investors who are the co-owners of their corporations. It is not surprising then that a comparison of 157 different health insurance plans for both regular buyers and for seniors revealed few really significant increases in the benefits available.

The principal differences were in the deductible features. If the deductibles were lower, the benefits were fewer or the premiums were higher. It adds up to a formula of six on one side and a half dozen on the other. In the end the plans must "balance out" premiums against possible benefit payments, with the law of probabilities as expressed in actuarial tables governing the amount and duration of the disbursements.

Some idea of the amounts of money involved may be had from the latest available figures released by the Health Insurance Institute in New York City.

United States voluntary health insurance organizations received $9.3 billion in premiums in 1963. This included subscriptions from Blue Cross, Blue Shield, and other hospitalization and surgical plans. It represented a 12 per cent increase in health insurance premiums over the previous year. These same organizations paid out $7.1 billion in benefits.

Americans spent $21.9 billion for medical care or an amount equal to 6 per cent of the money they spent on all of their personal needs. Per capita health expenditures grew from $91 in 1957 to $119 in 1962. It is expected that the figure will increase to $150 by 1970.

In direct payments to physicians Americans spent $6.3 billion in 1962—a 110 per cent increase over 1952. It should be remembered, however, that in that decade between censuses our population increased rapidly too. In effect, this spread those dollars over more physicians who were caring for more patients. In that same period there was a proportionate increase in the amounts spent on medicines and medical appliances. In 1962 it was $5.5 billion.

Exclusive of those admitted to federal facilities, 24,307,000 Americans were admitted to hospitals for treatment for relatively short periods. Expressed in terms of general medical care it means that we Americans paid nearly $22 billion for such services in 1962 and the figure is expected to increase to more than $40 billion by 1970.

In the Consumer Price Index issued by the U. S. Labor Department's Bureau of Labor Statistics, increased medical care expense for the study period amounted to nearly three times more than the money spent on housing, twice as much as was spent on transportation and personal care, four and a half times as much as was spent on food, and five times as much as the money spent on apparel.

There can be little doubt that, in the future, as all costs tend to increase, the cost of our insurance protection will tend to rise too. While older people can expect only a negligible increase in their life spans because of medical advances and the successful war on epidemic diseases, the younger people may expect substantially longer life spans. This will inevitably increase the possibilities for the incidence of many of the minor ailments that may be covered under health insurance plans. If more people produce the possibility of more such infirmities, this added expense will be reflected in the law of probabilities and inevitably in the cost of protecting one's family against them.

One of the most interesting new insurance plans is the private one (being reinsured by Blue Cross) offered by all of Ross Cortese's Leisure World retirement communities.

Cortese's operation is now larger than the combined efforts of all other retirement community developers in the world. And in many ways it is the most complicated. In order to better understand the potential for service that lies in his concept if and when he is able to turn it to reality (and much of it is already) it might be well to examine the Tinkers-to-Evers-to-

Chance structure of the operation . . . an operation, by the way, in which very little is left to chance.

The Rossmoor Corporation, a conventional construction company of huge proportions, finds land and plans the Leisure World retirement cities. At this point the Cortese-initiated, nonprofit Golden Rain Foundation contracts with the Rossmoor Corporation to build a Leisure World complex for it. Once this agreement is made, the nonprofit Golden Rain Foundation contracts with a third Cortese-inspired corporation known as New Horizons, Inc., to handle the sales to the public.

The entire taxpaying-tax-exempt-taxpaying chain reaction has received the approval of the Bureau of Internal Revenue and it has also received the unstinting praise of the Federal Housing Administration under whose little-used Section 213 this gigantic undertaking is insured. Since the FHA is the one government bureau that actually seems to earn its own keep, an operation such as Cortese's figures prominently in its own profit and loss statements.

As of February 28, 1965, there were six Leisure Worlds either in operation or planned and ready to start in the United States alone. Another has been contracted for in Lugano, Switzerland, and an eighth is nearing the final planning stage in Italy, whence Mr. Cortese's forebears emigrated.

The *modus operandi* of Cortese's medical plan is simplicity itself and the method of extracting the money to pay for it is relatively painless so far as the insured is concerned. Each buyer in a Leisure World purchases a share of stock in the co-operative in which his home is located. Approximately $34 of the total monthly charge is allocated to medical insurance premiums. The premium covers one or two occupants of the living unit. It covers up to 80 per cent of the cost of treating a number of specified ailments and is probably the broadest health insurance coverage available today. Even so, this plan, too, has its loopholes, its exceptions, and its exclusions dictated by what has come to be accepted as basic "good insurance" practice. The decision as to when this particular medical care plan ends is left to the Leisure World medical staff.

Since the six Leisure Worlds now operating or about to be will have a combined total of around 100,000 living units it takes very little figuring to arrive at a gross premium income to the Cortese-inspired, nonprofit Golden Rain Foundation of some $40,800,000 a year when all of the communities are built and operating to capacity. This is an impressive sum. In time it is possible that approximately 170,000 Leisure World residents may find comprehensive health insurance protection under such a potential premium income.

For the time being, however, a vast amount of the gross revenues will be spent to ensure the construction of at least five modern hospitals, clinics, and nursing homes. Nursing-home care is *not* included in Cortese's plan.

As one official put it, "If they need that, they are on their own! We'll provide the facilities but they must pay for their use."

Conceivably, when the medical facilities have been paid for and the entire organization has had an opportunity to accumulate some operating experience, the premium charges for this comprehensive care may be reduced. This is the announced objective of the Cortese organization, whose officials seem quite sincere in their efforts to bring medical and surgical protection for senior citizens in the Leisure Worlds down to the absolute minimum.

What the effect of Medicare will be is a matter for speculation. It is possible that persons who must subscribe to a private health insurance plan as a mandatory condition of residence in a Leisure World may also have to pay for medical care through payroll deductions and employer contributions.

Since the minimum admission age to the Leisure World complexes is fifty-two, many of the residents may be still active in the economy and merely using the ten to thirteen years before retirement as a period of emotional and economic adjustment to full retirement living.

Anyone who has seen the facilities that Cortese has provided for the amusement of his leisure-oriented residents will perhaps feel that no such period of adjustment is necessary, that on the contrary most will want to take the plunge forthwith. Indeed, that was the attitude of the majority of the residents at Seal Beach, California, Cortese's pioneer Leisure World. On the basis of his experience there certain changes have been made in the medical plan. (In the beginning it paid 100 per cent of the benefits and residents abused it.) And certain improvements have been made in the planning and design of the recreation facilities and the residences.

The function of the tax-exempt, nonprofit Golden Rain Foundation was of special interest in these investigations. At the outset the Golden Rain concept seemed to differ in practical application from the church-oriented organizations that serve the same general function in providing shelter, medical care, and recreation for retirees.

First, despite its umbilical connection at birth, the Foundation is a separate entity. Second, while it is a nonprofit organization and therefore eligible for certain definite tax advantages under state and federal law, it is for practical purposes the creation of the taxpaying Rossmoor Corporation on the one hand and the taxpaying New Horizons sales organization on the other.

The Golden Rain Foundation exists then in a rather special environment. Though it makes no direct contribution other than property taxes, it is, nonetheless, the fountainhead from which millions of dollars in taxes flow into the economy through the corporations that conceived it and gave it life.

It remains to be seen whether or not an approach to health insurance protection such as the one being undertaken by the Golden Rain Foundation will actually result in a substantial increase in security for those who are in a position to take advantage of it.

No disservice is implied in pointing out that for all its well-intentioned objectives it is still a plan designed to provide its greatest service for the relatively affluent elderly who will comprise the citizenry of these new retirement communities. According to officials of New Horizons, the sales organization for Cortese, the average net worth of the residents of the new Laguna Hills Leisure World is approximately $125,000 or about ten times greater than the median figure arrived at in Washington. (It is interesting to note that this net worth figure is very near that of our two sample families, A.L. and Z.K., in Chapter 1.)

To those who cry havoc and claim that Ross Cortese is going to disrupt the politics, the economy, and the social structure of the country there should be some reassurance in the fact that for all the grandiose scale of his dream it seems unlikely that he will be able to provide Leisure World living for much more than $2\frac{1}{2}$ per cent of the theoretical six million middle- to upper-income retirees that research indicates will be able to afford such accommodations, recreation, and comprehensive health insurance protection.

To paraphrase the oft-affirmed contention of many a western prospector, "Thar's a lot more gold left in them thar ills than's ever been took out!"

15

THE RETIREMENT CITY THAT SCARED A TOWN OUT OF ITS WITS

No matter where they spring up these large and largely self-sufficient retirement communities seem to send civic shivers through adjacent towns. In New Jersey, in Florida, in Maryland, in California, in Texas, in Oregon—the reactions have been essentially the same. We mortals are easily angered by the accusation that we resist progress and the advent of something new. And still, as soon as we are confronted by an innovation that threatens to change the comfortable or familiar status quo we greet it with skepticism or prejudice.

Del Webb, Ross Cortese, Boswell-Alliance, the Mackle Brothers, General Development, all the major creators of such communities have had to meet a constant barrage of criticism from those who fear the presence of a large concentration of elderly persons nearby. These fears are largely centered in two areas—a fear that the elders will upset the political balance and that they will also disrupt the social and economic balance of the community. So far these fears seem entirely unfounded. More than that, it would seem that if an established community plans carefully and incorporates within its limits one of these major retirement developments, it may reap advantages far beyond the purely financial rewards, which can be considerable.

Del Webb's Sun City in Arizona is too far from Phoenix to have any acute suburban effect on it. And still when the project was announced it was not difficult to find otherwise thoughtful persons predicting that the enterprise was doomed to failure and that many of the elderly citizens of Sun City doubtlessly would end up "on the city." They meant, of course, "on public assistance in Phoenix."

No such thing happened there or will it. If there has been any effect on adjacent towns it has been generally good, not only through increased publicity for the general area but also in increased revenues of all sorts.

A sad example of what built-in prejudice can do to a major community into whose trading area a new retirement city has come may be seen in the action of a militant group in the City Council of Laguna Beach, California, which is about fifty miles south of Los Angeles on the Pacific coast.

Ross Cortese's Leisure World at Seal Beach, less than twenty miles north of Laguna Beach, was already under way in 1962 when officials of the Rossmoor Corporation made informal contact with the Laguna Beach Council to sound out that body's attitude on possible annexation of Leisure World at Laguna Hills, just five miles to the east on the inland side of the coastal range.

The new retirement community wanted annexation in order to implement zoning and sewers. Under Cortese's proposal the city of Laguna Beach would have provided fire and police protection and a building department to approve construction and grant permits. The new Leisure World in return would have provided all of the physical buildings and equipment and in addition would have paid for its own water and sewer system and would have paid for all of the maintenance of the streets in the community with the exception of the main connecting road to Laguna Beach, then, as now, under county jurisdiction.

Laguna Hills had an enthusiastic champion in Laguna Beach's talented professional city manager, Jay Mercer. Mercer argued eloquently, pointing to the experience of Seal Beach in an attempt to convince a dissident minority in the council. In the end the battle grew so bitter that Mercer, a

former Navy jet pilot and to some a better scrapper than dip-
lomat, resigned in protest and was immediately offered a top
position with the Cortese organization.

Cortese's interests withdrew their informal request for annexation and established their own community. When completed it will have three times the population of Laguna Beach,
one of the possibilities that frightened certain citizens into such
an emotional state that they were alleged to have been inca-
pable of cool, self-serving judgment.

Most of the problems that the cautious council members
envisioned have not materialized anywhere else. Neither are
they likely to. Members of the school board were afraid that a
majority of oldsters would vote against expanding the school
system.

"They don't have any kids," the argument went. "Why
should they vote tax money or bonds for something they have
no interest in?"

At the city of Seal Beach, to which the first Leisure World
is an annexed suburb, forward-looking City Manager John
Williams had this to say:

"These older people at Seal Beach Leisure World voted
overwhelmingly for school bonds even though they do not use
the facilities at all!"

Another fear-engendered argument against annexation often
voiced in the Laguna Beach City Council was this:

"These old people are dangerous. A clever politician can
build them into pressure groups that can swing elections! The
Golden Rain Foundation will own them financially and politically, and before long Cortese's crowd will be running Laguna
Beach!"

Residents of Leisure World-Seal Beach outregister the residents of the city of Seal Beach by three to one and just the
opposite is true.

Certainly there are influential groups within the cooperatives
in Leisure World, but they have shown absolutely no disposition to listen to any proposals that might give them a selfish

advantage over the rest of the community. They are proud of their affiliation with Seal Beach and they show it.

"These senior citizens have displayed an unusually high degree of civic responsibility," said John Williams. "Their political behavior is far more responsible than the average—much fairer." Mr. Williams attributes this to the temperance and wisdom of age.

"We would do them a great disservice if we succumbed to the fiction that the older people among us are not capable of making sound decisions."

But these "bogey men" fears seem real enough when they are able to place a city such as Laguna Beach in the anomalous position of wanting to maintain the status quo while being strangled to death spacewise by surrounding communities whose annexation it has spurned.

A new city council appears to have taken a much more forward-looking attitude. But it is too late to woo Laguna Hills Leisure World back into the fold.

Very rarely, if ever, has there been such a fine opportunity to study the changing character of the American community complex as exists in these two instances. Responsible officials of any community who wish a detailed case history could hardly do better than to talk with City Manager John Williams of Seal Beach and former City Manager Jay Mercer of Laguna Beach. These two young men are important pioneers in a whole new sphere of human and political relations.

Unlike the new Leisure World communities that are now building, the first one at Seal Beach has no major hospital of its own and must rely on existing facilities in nearby towns.

The possibility that such might be the case at Laguna Hills Leisure World was also one of the many groundless fears that seized certain members of the Laguna Beach City Council.

"Cortese hasn't built anything but a clinic at Seal Beach. How do we know that he'll build that big hospital he's talking about at Laguna Hills? That may be just promoter talk. We haven't enough beds at our own South Coast Community Hospital now!"

As a Laguna Beach city councilman and Realtor, William Lambourne (not a member of the dissident council) said, "The plain truth is that our city council did not go into it far enough. The members raised a lot of theoretical arguments that turned out to be wrong. Laguna Beach has made a grave mistake."

Just how grave such a mistake may turn out to be is evident in still more experience gained by Seal Beach.

"One of the arguments used by the opponents of annexation here," explained John Williams, "is the one that older people with fixed incomes are frugal and do not spend money. Our experience shows the contrary to be true.

"In Leisure World during the 1963 fiscal year, the residents contributed only about twenty-five per cent of our property tax. In the 1964–65 fiscal year, the figure came out forty-three per cent of the total assessed valuation . . . nearly double."

On the subject of state taxes Mr. Williams said, "All of the state subventions will amount to eleven dollars a person this year [1964]. Six dollars is earmarked for major street systems which in effect frees other money in our budget for civic improvement. In addition, as the direct result of annexing this first Leisure World the City of Seal Beach has realized a forty per cent increase in sales taxes over 1962 and it will increase substantially each year."

The former Laguna Beach city manager had figures worked out that indicated conservatively that his city would have profited far more than Seal Beach from such an annexation—and without having to supply more than a minimum of municipal services to the new community.

"We could have been one of the richest and most progressive little cities in the entire nation," Mercer said unhappily, "if those particular council members had just roused themselves long enough to see what was happening around them. Laguna Beach is trapped now unless a new council takes a more aggressive and realistic attitude and begins annexing unincorporated communities that are in the natural sphere of its influence."

Critics point out that some inequities exist in these annexations of senior communities. John Williams acknowledged this.

"We have to levy the same tax rate against them as we do in other parts of Seal Beach," he said, "and we must do this without offering these older people all of the services to which they are entitled. We find them understanding and we are now working on ways to adjust these inequities."

One of the more persistent arguments advanced against Ross Cortese by the cities to which his Leisure Worlds are adjacent (excepting Seal Beach) stems from a fear that he is building too much too quickly . . . that his dream cities will collapse of their own weight.

"Cortese's overbuilding his market," some observers warned. "If these things flop there will be hell to pay clear across the country. Millions of dollars will be lost and thousands of old folks will be displaced!"

On the face of it the argument does not hold up. If the thousands of elderly persons were already in a Leisure World the economic structure of the community itself would be its own best insurance against any such failure or dislocation.

As for the argument that Cortese may overbuild his market, that seems unlikely also. On the basis of his announced 100,-000 units in the United States he would be supplying housing, recreation, and medical facilities for approximately 170,000 of the theoretical, and probably actual, six million persons in the middle- to upper-income brackets of the age sixty-five and over group and less than ½ per cent of the more than twenty million seniors age fifty-two and over, a very substantial segment of whom are prime prospects for Cortese.

All in all it would seem that no city has anything to fear from an adjacent retirement community providing it is located after thorough research as to market need, availability of the various civic facilities, and providing the promoters are ethical men and that the communities are well financed.

This exploding older population is growing more affluent as the years pass. Not only Social Security but union pension funds, retirement plans, and insurance plans are going to give a large segment of our population both more leisure time—an average of fourteen years after retirement at age sixty-five— and many billions of dollars more in spendable income. They must live somewhere. Men of great imagination and ability are going to compete for this growing market. It is not likely that any one of them can monopolize it in a lifetime despite the enthusiasm and optimism of the loyal supporters of one faction or another.

On the basis of the experience in Seal Beach these new retirement communities, properly conceived and managed, can be a blessing. John Williams confirmed this by pointing out that not only do the elderly citizens spend a greater proportion of their incomes but they also enrich the community by taking an active and constructive part in its affairs.

It is a fallacy to think of them as they are so often depicted in the enticing retirement-community ads—a group of gaudy-shirted, straw-hatted shuffleboard players who do little but grin self-consciously into the camera. Those who represent our seniors in a state of perpetual euphoria not only do them a great disservice but they do our country a great disservice as well by fostering both here and abroad an impression that is manifestly false.

16

CUPID'S LAST STAND

One waggish adviser suggested this chapter be titled "Sex and the Single Grandmother" and that it be left a blank page. Obviously this pessimist has been misinformed. The facts show that for an increasing number of single women in their later years—widows predominately—some measure of economic and emotional security is possible through remarriage.

The Department of Health, Education and Welfare, in pursuit of information on the aging, produced some figures on the incidence of romance among our elders that are encouraging.

A decade was studied (1949–59) and the results showed more than a glimmering of hope. For instance, while the total number of marriages of all ages was some 5 per cent less in 1959 than in 1949, the number of marriages among all older persons increased by more than one third. Moreover, marriages of older persons in which both bride and groom were over age sixty-five showed the largest numerical increase and the largest proportionate increase.

Though there are too few figures upon which to base any predictions of a fundamental change in the romantic pattern of our elders there is certainly some evidence that Cupid has made some significant gains in recent years in the matter of alleviating loneliness.

There are several reasons for this. Many of the couples who get married have been married before. One partner to the new union—often both—may have survived a previous mate. Some were victims of divorce. These latter appear to be the pioneer victims of our changing moral pattern immediately following World War I during the prohibition era.

Another reason may have to do with the growth of age-integrated communities such as those General Development is expanding in Florida in which a large percentage of the population falls in the senior citizen bracket.

In these communities when one partner dies there is a greater opportunity to meet potential partners of the same general age and economic bracket. Because of the very specific appeal of such communities it seems reasonable to expect a unanimity of interests, too, an aspect of marital compatibility that takes on added importance with the passing years.

It is difficult for a researcher to ferret out these possible romances. Older people are much more prone to open discussion of affairs other than romantic ones. When confronted with a question the women become more bashful than a self-conscious teen-ager in the throes of her first love affair. Certainly no bride could be more nervous than the one of sixty-five or more who is about to be rescued from the loneliness of widowhood. When asked why this was, one of them replied with unusual candor, "Relief is one reason—and then there is fear —and guilt."

Then she went on to explain, "I certainly didn't look forward to spending the rest of my life as a widow. You see I am completely alone. On the other hand I really don't know too much about this new man. He seems wonderful . . . and he's alone too . . . but then you never know. And of course, I always said when my first husband died that I would never ever marry again—that I just couldn't see myself sharing a bed with another man. That was sort of a pledge I made to my husband when I buried him. I guess I've broken that now," she added a bit ruefully, "but I know he'd want me to be happy."

(Note: Widows contemplating remarriage would do well to

discuss with their lawyers the possibility of lost benefits and the effect of same on the new financial position.)

Several of the women used the same rationalization. "I'm sure my first husband would want me to marry again rather than spend my last years in loneliness."

As for the grooms, in most instances they seemed remarkably calm, even complacent—and a touch smug, too—as though they were conferring something of a favor on their new brides. In short, they seemed very much aware that from their point of view they were enjoying the advantages of a "buyers' market."

In the retirement homes that require a minimum entrance age of sixty-five these romantic alliances are sealed, solemnized, and celebrated as major social functions. They become the occasion of widespread rejoicing and very little overt envy, though certainly if the groom is at all presentable there must be a strong undercurrent of the old "I wonder what on earth he sees in her?" attitude. (Often, too, these unions are widely exploited by the retirement community's publicity department.)

These potential December brides really get shaken by the pealing of the wedding bells in the newer retirement communities. Minimum age requirements are lower, hence the number of couples still living together is higher. Also, among the single persons the number of widows is proportionately higher. Weddings—any wedding involving one of their neighbors—really involves them emotionally.

Just as the late Dr. Kinsey found it necessary to interpret the answers to his questions to compensate for a tendency on the part of some to fib a bit on very personal answers, so must anyone investigating the love life, or lack of it, in the Leisure Worlds and Sun Cities adjust his too.

The lonely women are younger in these particular places and hence more apt to have had less time to adjust to their widowhood. As a consequence the ever-present reminders of the security and companionship of marriage have a more unsettling effect on them than on the more seasoned widow. In many respects these lonely ones are the most in need of companionship and the least able to accept it, particularly if their love for the departed mate was a profound one. This latter condition seems true of both widows and widowers.

At Kern City, California, Robert G. Bennet, retired Vice-president and Assistant Treasurer of the Spencer-Kellogg Company, international vegetable-oil refiners, shed a great deal of light on the problem from a widower's viewpoint.

"I've been an active man with the company since 1916," he said. "I always got the interesting and the tough assignments. My wife and I traveled and lived all over the world. We had a good life filled with a lot of adventure. And it was a very rich one too—with five children and fifteen grandchildren. And then Mrs. Bennet died—in 1959. That was nearly seven years ago," he said quietly, "and I'm still like a chicken without its head."

Mr. Bennet lives in a very comfortable condominium apartment in Kern City. He has fixed it up with some of the things from his old home and has done some redesigning in the kitchen and halls to make the place a little more convenient for his sort of bachelor living.

"I fix a few meals here," he explained, "but if I had to cook for myself I'd starve to death! But I've made arrangements with a widowed lady next door to cook for me. It works out real well for both of us."

Mr. Bennet then moved on to the various retirement communities he'd looked at before choosing his present home. "They were good in most respects," he said, "but I didn't want to get caught up in one of these forty thousand population places. I like the small-town suburban atmosphere here—and I like the sun."

Like many other men at these places Mr. Bennet has found that a golf course at his front door has turned him into an indefatigable player. "I like the game now. I get out every day—summer or winter!"

To a question about the possibility of remarriage, he gave this answer:

"I don't ever expect to be roped!" He was emphatic on the point. "Every once in a while some preacher will come around and say, 'Bennet, I want you to meet this widow. I buried her husband and she is one of the finest ladies I know.'"

Mr. Bennet snorted. "When that happens I have just one answer for them. I say, 'I'm giving you fair warning, friend. Don't you ever dare bring that woman into my house! I'm happy the way I am. I like it this way!'"

Mr. Bennet was almost convincing. But like others he seemed to protest a trifle too loudly.

Our conversation rambled over a number of events in Mr. Bennet's interesting life. It even included one episode in which he was captured and held for ransom by Chinese bandits on the Yangtse River in 1934.

Suddenly it was time for supper and Mr. Bennet's widow friend from the adjoining apartment knocked at the door. He insisted we stay and meet her.

When one uses the expression "widowed lady," there seems to be a universal tendency to picture her as something akin to Whistler's Mother. So we were hardly prepared for Mrs. Frances Redmond.

Though presumably old enough to qualify for the minimum entrance age of fifty at Kern City, Frances "Tottye" Redmond looked a good ten years younger. She was dressed in an attractive pink-cotton sunsuit that revealed a figure most twenty-year-olds would have coveted. She was blond, trim, and lovely —the sort of a woman men turn to admire and women look at with envy. There was a sweetness and gentleness about her that attracted one immediately.

Mrs. Redmond had been a widow for two and a half years and had decided to move out to Kern City to get away from old surroundings in Los Angeles. At the time of the interview she had been in Kern City a relatively short time. But she confessed that she enjoyed it.

"It is like a country club here," she said. "I'm learning to do a lot of things that I've not had time or inclination to do before."

Mrs. Redmond's sister and brother-in-law have joined her in Kern City. "They visited 'Tottye' and liked it so well here that they have decided to come and join us," explained Mr. Bennet.

One comes to recognize the look of hurt and loneliness in the eyes of these persons who have lost their mates. Sometimes it never quite leaves. After two and a half years there was still a trace of sadness in Mrs. Redmond's eyes.

It would be presumptuous to make any predictions about the lives of any of the men and women who were willing to discuss the problems of adjusting to retirement and loneliness. But certainly one might hazard a guess that for those still vital and attractive men and women there is real hope that new associations and new interests may also result in a new and fruitful life.

But the watchword seems to be "caution!" As one perennially defensive bachelor in Washington put it, "Women need a man real badly at a time like that—but they're not fit company for one. A man would be a fool to get serious about a widow whose eyes weren't dry yet! He'd be getting measured in every possible way against the dead husband. You can't win a contest like that!"

Of course it is not entirely unlikely that such a widower might be indulging in a few comparisons of his own, from which no middle-aged bridal candidate could hope to emerge a winner.

The consensus seems to follow the course of common sense: Don't go rushing into any new relationships of a permanent nature until you have made the cleanest possible break with the past. New needs may, one day, override old memories. If there has been more than one previous marriage for both parties to a December romance then the period of adjustment is not apt to be quite so long.

Instead of the wedding march, one whimsical older couple

who, collectively, had been through six previous marriages, insisted that the organist play a popular hit of some years back entitled "Everything's Been Done Before." It was widely conceded that this marriage had a good chance to work.

There are few more dependable sources of inside personal information than a good bartender. And one of the most popular *money magnets* in these new retirement cities is a restaurant-bar, often on the premises but seldom more than a block from the main entrance.

At Sun City near Riverside, California, an unnamed bartender at the King's Inn was as able to talk as he was willing. "'Through Darkest Retirement with Gimlet and Screwdriver,' is what I'd call it," he said. "I don't know any psychiatrists, but I'll bet there ain't a one of them hears anything more than a bartender—not even a priest!"

Under questioning this bartender admitted that the duty was "tougher" and the tips were smaller at a retirement community than at most places. "I'll tell you why," he volunteered. "You see the one thing that these older folks learn fast around here is that if they spend a lot of time talking about their troubles—their ailments and the like—they get to be unpopular in a hurry. The one thing that their new neighbors don't want is talk about operations and sickness . . . 'organ recitals' they call them. They just don't want any part of them! So," he said with a resigned shrug, "guess who gets to listen to 'em." He mopped the bar top mechanically and added, "It's not that there's anything wrong with working in this particular place. It's great . . . the best. But because we have older people here —and a lot of single women—widows mostly—we get to be like father confessors or something. They get lonely and maybe they never have done much drinking so they don't know how to handle it. If one of them gets something on her mind she is very apt to order one too many drinks and then spill all over a sympathetic bartender. 'Sympathetic Sam,' that's me!"

To the question "Are they ever troublesome?" he replied, "If you mean troublesome like rough or on the make or something like that—never! Mostly they want to talk—to unload on someone. Sometimes they need a drink to get up courage enough to talk. Once in a while we have to help one home. Sometimes newspapers and magazines write about that but it isn't really a common problem."

Management had another opinion to add to the story. "We would not knowingly take an alcoholic into one of our places. Once in a while one slips through. But more often—and usually it is a woman—a resident will become alcoholic out of sheer boredom and loneliness. These unfortunates can create an awful lot of trouble.

"Some of them fasten themselves onto sympathetic married couples of their same age and become very difficult friends indeed. Occasionally one of them will try to break up a marriage.

"Their presence at social functions is most unsettling! At an ordinary public party, management or the hostess can ask a troublesome guest to leave. But we must be very careful in handling them in these retirement places because not only do we as management understand their problems and sympathize with them but so do most of their fellow residents. Too often their way of offering a suffering widow solace is to urge another drink on her in the name of good fellowship. It is the worst thing that one can do. These women need attention, and if drinking gets them sympathy they'll keep on drinking more and more to get it. When that starts you can just about figure they'll go down the drain. It is the most difficult problem we have to handle."

There seems little solid evidence that people who live in retirement communities drink more than average amounts of liquor simply because they have the time or the means or a reason to. On the contrary, there is a great deal more drinking at almost any public function that one can mention than there is at the usual social gatherings of the retired.

As indicated earlier, there is a lot of special-occasion drinking, usually "fancy" celebration drinks with emphasis on

alexanders, pink ladies, silver fizzes, and sloe gin fizzes. The
occasions are the obvious ones—birthdays, anniversaries, holidays, and so on.

But at three barbecues attended in these communities fewer
and weaker cocktails were served than one would be likely to
find at any summertime back-yard barbecue in any average
suburban development. The same was true of wines with meals
and of after-dinner highballs.

Until someone takes the trouble to make a "study" of the
drinking habits of our senior citizens it would seem safe
enough to say, on the basis of several hundred interviews in a
dozen states, that "soused" seniors are a very small minority—
but one capable of creating an unusual amount of trouble in
these compressed societies.

Whereas their difficulties would be met with a certain
amount of indifference in the average residential community,
the empathic understanding of those moderately bibulous
seniors who are coping with many of the same emotional problems causes them to overreact—to oversympathize—and therefore to reap the troublesome rewards of their compassion.

Some ill-informed widows have actually taken up residence
in retirement communities under the cruel delusion that they
will find an abundance of single men there from whose ranks
they may capture a mate. When they are confronted with the
sorry truth—that single women are in the majority—those who
lack the social graces and the competitive urge may retreat to
the bars.

"It's hard to say," observed the bartender. "But just offhand
I'd say that a woman who takes to drink because of troubles
here would most likely do the same thing no matter where she
was. I don't think people change much in these places."

This would seem to confirm many other observations including some made by our senior sage, Spike Bentley.

"Retirement and retirement places are not likely to change
people much," he said. "If they were hard to get along with
before, they'll be difficult in retirement. If they couldn't face

their problems in the business world, they'll not face them in retirement. If they were inclined to drink and gamble before, they'll probably carry those problems into retirement."

Mr. Bentley is no cynic. He likes people and understands them.

"Women in retirement are proud of having a husband left. A husband is not only a symbol of security but also of status. The widows outnumber them about three to one, I'd estimate. That means a person with a surviving mate belongs to the senior elite. That would be even truer in any community in which there is a concentration of older people."

In an effort to further verify with a body of evidence these sensible-sounding observations on senior behavior we visited a score of retirement communities and establishments and questioned residents. There was a unanimity of opinion that confirmed these earlier observations. No matter what part of the country we visited the cooperative seniors were in accord on the fundamental premise that neither the state of retirement nor the special environments created to accommodate the retiree could exert much influence on the fundamental behavior of any senior citizen. "Old people are the same people they were as young people—only more so," is the way one administrator put it.

This summation was borne out in areas where one might suspect younger behavior patterns would have changed. In the case of connubial jealousies it would seem that the "only more so" condition had grown even more acute.

A newly retired federal employee who wished to remain anonymous because of the fear of recriminations in his particular retirement city had this to say:

"Women in these places are proud of having their men left —and they are jealous too. Some of the widows around here are still quite young and good-looking and they are a real threat as some wives see it. A married man had better not get caught sneaking one too many looks! Of course," he added, "if a fellow wants to get into trouble around here he can find ways to do it—I mean trouble with single women. But I always say that if you aren't aiming to get into a mess like that you won't. Even at this age it still takes two to tango!"

. . . and three to make a triangle. But it would appear that such triangles do not often get made in the Leisure Worlds, Sun Cities, and Friendly Valleys of this country.

When asked why this low incidence of autumnal infidelity one wag replied, "Because a fellow who was that kind of a swinger probably dropped dead from it before he reached retirement age!"

Masking the deep misgivings and downright fright of so many seniors is a certain ironic humor. A characteristic example may be found in the definition of a lucky widow who does manage to beat the odds and find romance. She is said to be "on her last lap."

17

"OH, BITTER DICTUM!"

In the months since the first chapter of *The Retirement Trap* was written, the final chapter has been written to one of those two true stories.

Mr. Z.K. has died of cancer. Mrs. Z.K. is going through the soul-wrenching adjustments to widowhood that have already been experienced by roughly six and one half million wives in their middle years.

Perhaps some readers will be tempted to label many of these stories maudlin, to charge overt sentimentality and overdramatization in the retelling. And still, overdramatization of the plight of most of these women is quite impossible.

That special quality of endurance with which God has endowed the childbearing half of the human species is never more evident than during this period of adjustment. Problems that would cause strong men to quaver are faced by these women—faced for the most part with such valor and with such absence of self-pity that those who complain of lesser troubles should be silenced by shame.

Mrs. Z.K.'s fears were not for herself after her husband's death. "I knew it had to be," she said, "but there is always a little corner of hope in the heart. So when it happens—finally —you feel so many things. Zach suffered. So you thank God that his suffering is over. But even when you expect death, there is a shock." Mrs. Z.K. retreated into herself briefly. Then she continued to respond to a difficult questioning.

"I know this shock is affecting me," she said. "I know it will be a long time before I stop waking up in the night like I have for thirty-five years and being shocked to find he's not there any more.

"The children have been marvelous to me. They took all of Zach's things and stored them. But even so, I find some little thing he's tucked away and I remember why he did it—and what he said at the time—and it's almost like he's here again. Those are the worst times.

"I'll tell you something else, too—if I look outside and see our oldest boy drive up with my daughter-in-law, I get a shock. From a distance Marvin looks just like his father looked for so many years. I guess the only thing to do is to keep busy—to let time pass. It wouldn't be so hard if it didn't seem so empty. Even with my grown children—it is empty, believe me. But I thank God for them—not for the help they give—they paid for the funeral—over a thousand dollars—because the money is almost gone now—but I thank God that I'm not alone like so many older women I know."

Mrs. Z.K. closed her eyes and shook her head gently. "For them every day must be such a torture! I had sympathy for them before, God knows—but now I *really* understand!"

Anyone who can witness the anguish of newly imposed widowhood and brand it melodrama is simply scoffing at a human condition that he lacks the courage to face. There are such persons. They are the same ones who counseled us against a book devoted to the human side of retirement.

"Leave that to the gerontologists and professors," they said. "Nobody wants to be reminded that he's getting old or that it isn't going to be easy. People don't want to think about it!"

Superficially that counsel is correct. But many persons were candid enough to say that they had deferred planning for their retirement simply because they had not realized how quickly time was passing.

An executive in charge of the retirement program for one of the large electronics corporations stated recently that the biggest problem his staff faces is urging young employees to begin planning their eventual retirement early enough to make possible a comprehensive program. "They simply don't realize how little time there is left—even if they are still in their mid-thirties," he said.

A typical attitude is the following statement taped during an interview with a young electronics engineer who is thirty-three:

"What the heck!" he exclaimed with some indignation, "I'm not ready to start thinking about going to pasture yet! My youngest child is only three. Wait until I get the kids in college. Then I'll start worrying about a retirement plan."

The following is from another interview with a man of fifty-three—just twenty years older:

"I hadn't planned to retire for ten years yet. But these coronary symptoms popped up twice and the doctor said that my only chance was to get out from under the load. We'll be able to get by all right—unless one of us gets hit badly. But I sure wish that I had started planning on emergencies like this when I was in my thirties! We'd have been well fixed now!"

The man whose infallible "hindsight" is thus revealed was not chosen because his situation is unique, but rather because it is so commonplace. He and his wife will get by—if—. Said one of his fellow gamblers, "The name of *this* game is, 'You Bet Your Life'!"

Depending upon the figures used, the odds in favor of a lonely widowhood for most middle-aged married women are about three-to-two. Some figures would place the odds at three-to-one in favor of widowhood by age sixty. None of the experts interviewed would hold out much hope that the figures would stabilize, much less decrease, in an economy that demands more and more of responsible employees at all levels.

More leisure time for workers may eventually tend to reduce that strain. But not so for the executive who cannot "shut down the machine" and walk away from it.

"There may come a time when socio-economic changes will mitigate some of the harshness our system presently imposes upon older persons. Such a day is theoretically possible," said Dr. Donald Kent. Then he went on to sum up, "But we are faced with the fact that our older population is increasing at more than a thousand persons a day. The majority of them are going to require assistance beyond that presently available under private and government programs. We are going to have to take care of these people within the concept of our free society. That means providing for them without diminishing their status or threatening their dignity."

Dr. Kent pointed out that one of the great problems in accomplishing this is a psychological one. "The qualities of age are no longer valued," he said, reiterating his central premise. "The result is that age does not respect itself because our society no longer respects age."

The reluctance encountered may well proceed from this first cause. Resistance to retirement planning was evident in scores of interviews with men in their prime business years, men from both management and labor whose economic status is such that well-planned, conscientiously pursued retirement programs could result in financial security, perhaps even in the event of catastrophic illnesses.

The attitude was expressed in language similar to that used by the thirty-three-year-old electronics engineer. In effect these men expressed their reluctance by saying, "Company [or union] benefits take care of all that. We'll be okay with our pensions and our Social Security checks. Besides, we've got group medical plans and our own investments too."

When one realizes how widespread this apathy is it is easy to understand the unhappy plight of so many widows. It is true, as it was in the cases of A.L. and Z.K. in Chapter 1, that the majority of these heads of families will have done more to ensure reasonable security in retirement than their fathers had done. But *reasonable security* in our time, when compared with what might have been termed such two or three decades ago, can be pitifully insufficient.

Incomes may vary and it may be possible for government bureaus to reduce such figures to averages. However, no computer has been, or likely will be, invented that will reduce to a common average the emotional upheaval that accompanies the death of a partner. At the center of that upheaval is the problem of security. Certainly not even total *material* security will ever be able to mitigate the sense of loss inflicted by the passing of a long-time mate. A very great portion of the burden has been lifted in those instances where the condition of widowhood has been ameliorated by sufficient means to enable the victims to continue living with dignity.

There is little question that congregate living such as that offered by many of the church-motivated, life-care retirement homes does much to alleviate loneliness for those who can afford such comforting. Widows comprise the majority of residents in such places. They start with two great things in common—the burden of their loneliness and sufficient means to share this particular social and economic status.

Activity programs attempt to substitute new group relationships for old family relationships where families no longer exist. As indicated earlier the lonely ones hasten to form new attachments and they do find some solace and emotional stability. But these comforts are available to and can be afforded by such a small segment of the total senior population that they are but a drop in the bucket.

This does not imply that to relieve the suffering of even one such older person is a negligible act. But it does imply that even the combined efforts of everyone interested in the problem thus far must be termed negligible when measured against the *ideal solution* which, in an economy as abundant as ours, may no longer be called theoretical.

A fraction of the cost of developing new atomic weapons, a fraction of the cost of protracted lunar explorations could all but wipe out the problem of caring for the needy elderly and the aged in this country. Some economists cringe when it is suggested that this, too, be undertaken on a top priority basis. Apparently forgetting the $40 billion potential, they base their arguments on the so-called lack of a dynamic market by which these expenditures may be returned to the economy in terms of additionally created wealth.

And still it was not possible to find a single economist who would give assurances that the billions spent on proving that the moon is not made of green cheese will be multiplied in our economy through the development of some sort of new "lunar market" à la Dick Tracy that will increase our gross national product. Brushing aside the urgency of providing for our exploding elderly population, they seek to reassure us that America's space expenditures are necessary to our international prestige and security.

The simple truth behind this apathy lies in the fact that there is little or no glamor or sense of adventure in exploring the dark side of our own planet's socio-economic problems. It is far more agreeable for those at the peak of life's energy and their own earning capacity to sublimate their responsibilities to the future in the far-out adventures of the space age.

To be forced to think about the condition of our own aging citizens is to be forced to think about one's own future problems. This has always been a distasteful duty for the young of any generation.

The problem will be solved someday because we are going to be forced to solve it—not only in this country but in all of the countries of the world. The population explosion is not an isolated phenomenon. It is an international crisis. Whether solutions be attempted through socialistic means, private industry and union collaborations that will provide security for most of this country's labor force, or through a combination of private and government effort, the problem will not truly be solved until each responsible citizen has the means to solve his own problem.

When that is accomplished, and there are many qualified persons who say that it is now possible under our free enterprise system, then we will surely have accepted the highest degree of individual responsibility and we will have taken the fullest advantage of the freedom of individual initiative implicit in our way of life.

This is not a Utopian dream. It is a hardheaded possibility. But it is hardly a *probability* yet for it implies a universal awareness of our moral and social obligations that presently are clear only to some sociologists and to an enlightened few in the ranks of industry on both sides of the "collar line."

Because President Kennedy and his advisers understood the growing national awareness of the problems of our exploding elderly population they chose to make it a major issue in the 1960 campaign. President Lyndon Johnson has made it a major objective of his administration. Medicare is an attempt to meet the predominant economic need of the elderly.

There is no single, simple solution, nor can there be, for there is no single problem to be attacked. One may speak of the problems of adjusting to retirement. But that is simply a categorical umbrella under which are huddled a great many related problems.

Dozens of agencies at all levels of government, the National Retired Teachers Association and the related National Association of Retired Persons, both founded by the remarkable Dr. Ethel Percy Andrus, and a small but dedicated group of citizens who comprise the National Council on the Aging, together with various local and regional housing authorities are tackling various aspects of the over-all need. Certain other groups, such as the Rochester Management Group in New York State, are working effectively to alleviate part of the burden that accompanies old age.

The housing authorities would seem to offer the best potential for helping in the lower-income brackets. But even here there is a tendency to concentrate on the problems of housing younger citizens, families unable to afford private housing because they have been displaced by highly controversial area redevelopment projects, and side-step once again the more urgent problem of the aged. Of the 1500 local housing authorities in the country only about three hundred of them are giving any significant attention to the housing needs of the elderly.

The major effort, then, is still being made by the church and fraternally motivated, nonprofit, tax-favored groups. But as we have seen, they have concentrated most of their effort on solving the not-so-urgent needs of the relatively affluent elderly.

Because it may appear to some that a deliberate attempt is being made to dwell unduly upon the activities of this church-associated group for the purpose of discrediting all such undertakings, it should be made clear that there are scores of nonprofit, tax-favored projects among Catholics, Protestants, Jews, and certain fraternal groups that are doing a splendid charitable work in providing the needy elderly with the physical and spiritual amenities necessary to a secure and dignified retirement.

But, as the Reverend Lawrence Upton has pointed out, too many such efforts are devoted to areas in which the needs are neither most numerous nor most urgent.

While there is certainly nothing legally wrong with providing a service where there is a demand, it would seem that a higher moral obligation should devolve upon those who, in the name of charity and with the advantages of lenient laws designed to expedite charitable work, are in a favored position to help. Many churchmen hope that conscience will prevail as the awareness of the problem grows and many of those now catering to the affluent elderly will broaden their concepts and find ways to provide care for those who cannot afford to pay sizable fortunes for admittance to comfortable surroundings and adequate care.

But again, there is the dilemma present in the difference between possibilities and probabilities. Only this time the order is reversed. It is probable that some of these church-motivated retirement homes may see the light and sincerely wish to widen the scope of their charity. But it is hardly possible that they will be able to do more than think wishfully, because the most elaborate of them are geared economically to such a high scale that if any significant percentage of their living space were to be assigned to elderly persons who could not afford the full tariff, management would face a financial disaster.

From time to time these institutions have been referred to as "tax-exempt" or "tax-favored." This distinction is made because in some cases they are quite literally exempted from all taxes. But there are a number of nonprofit retirement homes that do pay some local and state taxes. However, there seems never to be any question of income tax, for they are all exempted from such payments under the nonprofit provisions of both state and federal laws.

In the case of the elaborate institutions any attempt to force them to broaden their concepts of charity quite possibly would result in the need for more federal, state, and county tax forgiveness or direct assistance to enable them to function at all. The end would be to further increase the burden of the taxpayer.

Many a bitter argument can be started over the best means of bringing the increasing number of our needy elderly into a condition of security and dignity. Some say that an extension of Social Security is the answer. These people generally support the Medicare plan and deny categorically that it could be extended to cover younger persons until, in the end, it would amount to a form of socialized medicine.

Others say the ideal solution is for management to give labor broader benefits so that during a worker's productive years he or she may accumulate sufficient of these benefits to provide economic security from retirement to the grave. Many of these persons would penalize efficient management that must answer to stockholders while at the same time demanding that management "share the corporate wealth" with little or no control over the disposition of labor's end of those potential billions.

The nation's unions are already immensely wealthy. In more than a few cases they have an embarrassment of riches. And in many cases the unions themselves have become larger and more powerful than the businesses that sustain them. In case after case it has been shown in the nation's courts that some unions have abused their trusteeships. Millions of workers' dollars have been diverted to investments that have enriched a few of the powerful ones at the expense of the dues-paying rank and file. Multibillion-dollar funds lie around at the disposal of smart or favored investors while a needy former truck driver who has paid dues all of his adult life may be forced into an appeal for public assistance or into the clutches of a loan shark.

Certainly there are many unions that are models of responsibility. Organizations are associations of people and as such they reflect the dominant aspects of human nature. In the paradox that is human nature—in the brighter side of that duality —lies what hope there may be for truly effective help for the great mass of victims of The Retirement Trap.

Just as some may point an accusing finger at certain groups in the Teamsters' Union so may one point with pride to the I.L.G.W.U.'s enlightened retirement plan.

Just as some may look askance at certain nonprofit groups that operate under definitions of charity deliberately broadened by law to benefit them, so may one look with respect at the work being done by the Mormon Church, for instance, whose members are pledged to ensure their own security without public aid by a planned thrift program.

When catastrophic illness strikes and a Mormon is threatened with destitution he rarely appeals for outside help. Instead, he calls upon his bishop, who in turn calls upon the officers of his stake. Then the unfortunate one is cared for until he is self-sustaining again. The secret of this security is a consistent, realistic private plan of savings and an ingrained sense of personal responsibility.

The Jewish Homes for the Aged are models of self-sustaining service organizations. Though they are in the minority it is impossible to begin to list all of the deserving organizations, both religious and otherwise, that are effectively accepting the responsibility of caring for their own. But as long as the list may be, and as heartening, it is still but a small beginning on a great problem.

Hardly a person will be found who would deny that the richest and most productive economy the world has ever known is unable to solve the problems of its needy elderly. And still, when it was suggested that some sort of obligatory, retirement health insurance plan might be set up with industry and union cooperation that would not be payable under most circumstances until age sixty-five, an unholy howl went up.

"Look, friend! They are already deducting such and such an amount from my paycheck for Social Security, union dues, and what not. If they deduct any more there won't be any pay left to take home!"

When asked how many Irish sweepstakes tickets they purchased these same workers admitted that they contributed substantially to these "worthy causes." They also admitted (in the West) that they made at least one and sometimes two trips each year to "Vegas" or Reno. Also, they participated in a number of neighborhood or plant football, baseball, and basketball pools.

When these extracurricular expenditures were averaged, including the cost of trips to Las Vegas or Reno, it was found that these working men and women who said *another dollar or two of deductions would break them* were spending an average of $533 a year on such diversions. None of them would concede that even half of that amount put into some form of prepaid, retirement medical insurance would be a good investment against future problems. In effect what they said was this:

"By the time the government got through hiring people to take care of the money there wouldn't be anything left in it for us!" One might as well argue that by the time the Security Exchange Commission gets through administering stock transactions in this country there is nothing left for the broker or stockholder. It is a difficult task indeed to force a shaft of light through a closed mind!

Assumptions are dangerous, but it would seem a justifiable risk to assume that a sampling of attitudes taken in half of our states might represent a fair cross section of opinion on the matter of some form of retirement medical insurance administered by industry and labor under the regulation of an appropriate government body. The nation's insurance companies thrive under such regulation.

It was interesting to note, however, that the higher the level of the employee and the greater his responsibility in his firm, the more willing he was to give some thought to the possibility of some form of painless sacrifice at the payroll level in order to insure himself and his family against the financial devastation of catastrophic illnesses after retirement.

"Some plan like that—in addition to Social Security—might work," they agreed. In most cases they were willing to forego "a few martinis" if a chance existed that such a plan could be *initiated and administered by private industry*.

So, while both segments of our work force feared the alleged inefficiency of governmental control or administration of any such retirement health insurance plan, those who do not need it so urgently see reason in it and those who would most likely fall victims of The Retirement Trap don't want to face the facts —if it means a curtailment of their pleasures.

Elsewhere it has been suggested that this creative and infinitely versatile economy of ours is perfectly capable of meeting its problems within the framework of private enterprise. Any nation, a portion of whose work force can afford to spend $10 billion in three years in Las Vegas alone, would hardly seem to be in dire danger of making a major sacrifice were it decided to earmark still another modest portion of its gross paycheck for prepaid private retirement health insurance.

Those who disagree overlook the fact that *the sums spent*

on gambling are not spent in lieu of other recreational activities, they are spent in addition to family vacations, movies, sporting events, and holiday trips.

So it seems likely that we are destined to go on as we have been, swinging between the two poles, government paternalism on the one hand and on the other a still evident desire on the part of the average American to accept the responsibility for his own problems. Where that pendulum finally comes to rest will determine the nature and character of our American society for generations to come.

The roughly 1.5 million who will retire each year during the foreseeable future may look forward to living in one of the several conditions described in these pages. From the figures it is clear that only a small percentage of them will live in anything like the degree of comfort they enjoyed during their peak productive years.

The majority of elders will find retirement living both a severe material and emotional jolt, a time of trial when the trials of life should be over.

Social Security will help some 23 million of them. Private pensions averaging from 20 per cent to 40 per cent of pre-retirement incomes will help approximately 20 million—quite possibly many of the same. But even with Social Security and a pension, *fixed incomes both*, the pinch will be felt from the beginning. And it is not likely to lessen as all costs continue to rise—and none more spectacularly than those related to the maintenance of health. This is the one expense for the elderly that the law of probabilities says will be inescapable.

It is possible for our senior citizens with fixed incomes to conserve dollars by more careful budgeting in most areas. *But there is no shopping for bargains in good medical treatment or in first-class hospital care.* Indeed, the possibilities for such, if they ever did exist, will grow less and less likely as time goes on. This will not necessarily be the result of an arbitrary increase in the services of members of the medical profession, although living costs will exert some effect on medical payrolls too. Rather, these increases will be the direct result of technical advances in diagnosis and treatment.

In most industries and in many professions mechanization and automation can lower the unit cost of a product or a service by increasing the speed with which it may be produced or rendered. But in medical analysis and treatment the remarkable new tools and techniques being made available through our new technology have a tendency to make medical work more thorough and more exact. Because these techniques are complicated they require higher skills in those who use them. Being more complicated they often require more time to accomplish their work than the "by-guess-and-by-God" methods often resorted to in the medical profession only a generation or so ago.

So it would appear that our elderly, looking for more medical services for their fixed income dollars, are destined to look in vain for relief in this quarter. Whether this expense be merely an added burden or a tragic hardship, it is a common prospect for retired Americans everywhere.

From time to time in the past politicians and demagogues have tried to weld America's senior citizenry into a unified political force. Sometimes the attempts have met with moderate success at local and state levels. But the greatest difficulty heretofore has been the problem of reaching seniors on a national scale because they have been so scattered throughout the entire population.

But with larger and larger concentrations of retirees and the elderly living in their own communities it will become easier for someone with a plan to get at them.

This possibility need not become a thing to be feared as it was by the city of Laguna Beach, California. As was demonstrated by the dominant senior electorate at Seal Beach, California, retired citizens can be extraordinarily unselfish and politically responsible.

Because they, too, suffer from the shortcomings of human

nature there will always be an element among our elders who will vote for a "something for nothing" scheme. But the majority of our senior voters have come to understand that in government as in all other undertakings you get what you pay for. There are no free passes. *Somebody must pay*.

If in time our free society is able to devise some form of prepaid private retirement health insurance, paid for in weekly increments during a worker's productive years, the funds not available for health protection under most conditions until retirement at age sixty-two or sixty-five, it seems likely that chief support for it will come not from the younger workers who would rather shoot an extra dollar or two on the horses or the crap tables, but rather from the elders themselves who are in a position to understand the real value of such protection even though there may be little or no hope that their own generation will benefit greatly from it.

Much has been written about the condition of old age and the best means of coping with it. But few observations contain as much common sense as those of Cicero in 44 B.C.

Sometimes in imaginary dialogues—the fashion of the times —and sometimes in direct statement, this Roman sage covered almost every aspect of the problem. He summed up the philosophy of aging, activities for the old, consolations for lost strength, the pleasures of age, the joys of nature, the honors and faults, and finally, death and immortality.

In Michael Grant's brilliant translation the crystal-clear wisdom of this ancient and yet so modern man shines like a beacon. On the place of our elders in society, Cicero's logic is as pertinent today as it was two thousand years ago:

People who declare that there are no activities for old age are speaking beside the point. It is like saying that a pilot has nothing to do with sailing a ship because he leaves others to climb the masts and run along the gangways and work the pumps, while he himself sits quietly in the stern holding the rudder.

He may not be doing what the younger men are doing,

but his contribution is more significant and valuable than theirs.

Great deeds are not done by strength or speed or physique; they are the products of thought and character, and judgment. And far from diminishing, such qualities actually increase with age.

To emphasize his point Cicero pointed out that "the greatest states were overturned by young men and restored by the old." But nothing he said about age was more pertinent than his comment on self-respect. Today as in Cicero's time we are faced with a youth-centered society that tends more and more to relegate its elders to the social and economic scrap heaps.

Cicero pointed the way to emancipation for the elderly during the last year of his own life when he said, "Age will only be respected if it fights for itself, maintains its own rights, avoids dependence, and asserts control over its own sphere as long as life lasts."

Very soon now, and for the first time in the history of our country, our seniors will be numerous enough to form a political block. If these elders act in concert they can indeed assert control over their own sphere "as long as life lasts."

SPECIAL ACKNOWLEDGMENTS

The debt of gratitude owed to so many is implicit in the use of their names and their opinions in the main body of the text.

But in the hundreds of interviews in all parts of the United States and in the Bahamas where we looked into the matter of expatriot retirees and the possibilities for stretching fixed incomes through favorable exchanges we very quickly found ourselves in debt to scores of friendly persons, many of whom preferred to remain anonymous.

Should this book fall into their hands this will be inadequate but sincere thanks for helping sharpen our insight and for providing us with what was often painfully personal information.

Above and beyond those extraordinary services were the willing assistances from specialists in related fields whose generous cooperation helped us to round out what we believe to be the first general survey of retirement and its problems written especially for those who face their last and perhaps most difficult adjustment to the demands of our society.

It seems inevitable that despite care in keeping records in order to prevent the possibility, there will be some inadvertent omissions. Please know them for what they are.

Our deepest gratitude extends also to:

Walter L. Berdahl, Director of Advertising and Sales Promotion, General Development Corporation, Miami, Florida.

Robert M. Brumby, Vice President, Public Relations, Jack Tar Hotels, Grand Bahama Island.

Kenneth F. Brown, Executive Director, Tom Sawyer Village, Housing Authority, City of Reno, Nevada.

Dorothy M. Crippen, Executive Vice President, National Retired Teachers Association and American Association of Retired Persons.

Helen Holt, Special Assistant for Nursing Homes, Federal Housing Administration, Washington, D.C.

Marvin A. Kobel, Director of Public Relations, National Association of Underwriters, Washington, D.C.

John C. Lynsky, Director, Advertising and Sales Promotion, The Grand Bahama Development Company, Ltd., Miami, Florida.

Robert Moon, Vice President, New Horizons, Inc.

Gracie Pfost, Special Assistant, Federal Housing Administration, Washington, D.C.

Sidney Spector, Coordinator for Elderly Housing and Assistant Administrator, Federal Housing Administration, Washington, D.C.

Winifred E. Stone, Librarian, National Council on the Aging, New York City.

Gus Tyler, Assistant President, International Ladies Garment Workers Union, New York City.

Robert Waldron, Public Information Service, Health Insurance Institute, New York City.

George and Louise Welsh, Directors, Casa Romantica by the Sea, San Clemente, California.

Also we wish to especially thank A. C. Connelly, Sales Engineer, General Development Corporation, Miami, Florida, for his patience and enthusiasm in showing us firsthand the "Port Cities" and making possible numerous interviews with retirees.

And Harold (Hal) Hewett, Activities Coordinator and Public Relations Director and Lee C. Phillips, Project Manager, Kern City, Del E. Webb Corporation, whose unusual perceptiveness led us to a group of retired men and women with the gift of objectivity and the ability to communicate with researchers.

And our thanks to Jerry McLain, Vice President, Del E. Webb Corporation and to Wally McLain of that corporation for opening so many doors . . . and for doing so without restrictions.

And lastly our thanks to Frank V. McCullough, Vice President in Charge of the Disability Division of the Combined Insurance Companies of America, Chicago, Illinois, for confirming as potentially sound some of the conclusions arrived at by us concerning the desirability and the possibility of private industry using its inventive and sales genius to create and implement some form of prepaid retirement health insurance that would, in time, give older people adequate comprehensive coverage.

We do not imply, by the use of any material voluntarily provided for this work from any source, that those who cooperated necessarily agree with our personal conclusions as set forth in these pages. Where, in our opinion, any of the material freely given might, by its presentation, cause even the slightest embarrassment, we have deliberately refrained from identifying such persons by name and/or by profession.

Leland Frederick Cooley
Lee Morrison Cooley

Laguna Beach, California
June 1, 1965.